I Win, You Win

The essential guide to principled negotiation

Carl Lyons

A & C Black • London

First published in Great Britain 2007

A & C Black Publishers Ltd,
38 Soho Square,
London W1D 3HB

© Carl Lyons 2007

A CIP record for this book is available from the British
Library.

ISBN: 978-0-7136-7705-8

This book is produced using paper that is made from
wood grown in managed sustainable forests. It is natural,
renewable and recyclable. The logging and manufacturing
processes conform to the environmental regulations of the
country of origin.

Page design by Fiona Pike, Pike Design, Winchester
Typeset in Legacy 10.75/13pt
Printed in the United Kingdom by Bookmarque, Croydon

Contents

For Don and Janet Lyons, my parents, mentors and role models who through their example have taught me the power of integrity.

Acknowledgements

There are a number of people I want to thank for helping me in the writing of this book. Michele Baylis for her support, inspiration and belief; Fiona Pusey for generously sharing her knowledge and for some of the material in the communication chapters; Jason Melville for openly sharing his experiences and for the case study in Chapter 3; Lisa Carden at A & C Black for her belief in the project and her constant enthusiasm and support; Emma Harris at A & C Black for her patient and skilful editing. I also wanted to acknowledge those writers, mentors and students who have helped to shape and inspire my own practice and teaching over the years and whose influences can be clearly seen in this material; Roger Fisher, William Ury, G. Richard Shell, Chester Karrass and many others.

Introduction

Negotiation is the game of life. Whether you know it or not, you are negotiating all the time: with your kids, your partner, your boss or your clients. The truth is, we often don't get what we think we deserve in life; we get what we negotiate. You negotiate the cost of repairs with your plumber, whether your kids eat their vegetables, who does the dishes with your partner or a pay rise with your boss. Learning to negotiate skilfully can improve your income, your relationships and help you get significantly more out of your life. But the fact that people negotiate in many areas of their lives does not mean that it is done well.

Here we will describe a set of principles that will help apply a level of integrity to everything that you negotiate. The word integrity comes from the Latin root meaning 'wholeness'. This system is about being aware of the impact of our behaviour and decision-making at every level. It is about managing relationships in the long, as well as the short term and satisfying not only your own interests, but also the interests of those you are negotiating with. It is not about manipulating others to do something they don't want to do or being more powerful so that the other party succumbs to your needs.

Negotiating with integrity is worth doing, not out of some moral obligation to do what is right, but simply because it works. We negotiate with other parties only when we can get more from an agreement with them, than from the other options we have. Agreements are made only when you are able to satisfy the things that the other party wants as well as satisfying our own interests. In other words, if you approach negotiations by focusing solely on your own interests, your results will be inconsistent and seldom successful, and those agreements you do make are unlikely to produce harmonious, lasting relationships. Quite simply, if you don't satisfy the other party's needs as well as your own, then you won't make good agreements. If you pressurise, manipulate or force an outcome, often it will come back to you in some damaging way in the future. Former American president Jimmy Carter once said, 'Unless both sides win, no agreement can be permanent.'

These days we are doing business in a climate where our relationships are increasingly important and interconnected. There is more choice and competition than ever before in many sectors and whether we trust someone is often the deciding factor in where our business goes. Our expectations for our life are higher than they have ever been and that is exactly as it should be. In our work we increasingly want to be inspired and impassioned, not just turning up in order to pay the bills. In our social relationships, fewer of us are just satisfying the need for companionship or social expectation; we want to be fulfilled emotionally and spiritually. This is the right standard and possible for everyone to attain. However, raising expectations is only the first step. We also need to develop the attitude and skills that will deliberately create the things we want.

Negotiating with integrity is a system of actively getting what you want but at the same time building lasting relationships with those you are negotiating with.

I know there are negotiations we undertake where the quality or longevity of the relationship do not seem that important. However, even if you are negotiating with a plumber to get some repairs done on your house, how the negotiation is conducted will impact not only on the price, but also the efficiency and quality of work done. And because it's not that easy to get a good plumber these days you are also laying some solid foundations in case you need their services again in the future. In business I have managed complex, multi-million pound negotiations in a corporate environment dealing with other large organisations. Over the last few years I have also run my own companies, making agreements that may have been financially smaller and simpler than the corporate negotiations, but which had a much greater personal impact. In managing a property portfolio I have managed negotiations with agents and with tenants where the issues can become very personal and emotional. Whatever the circum-stances, how the relationship is managed has an impact on the outcome every time.

Even relationships that seem transient will often recur in our lives. I had a friend that was selling his house and had found an interested buyer. The survey indicated some issues that could have caused problems with the sale. My friend dealt with the problems quickly and efficiently and in a way that left everyone concerned feeling good about the completed transaction. About a year later, my friend, who is a self-employed consultant, pitched for an important contract. When he entered the negotiating room, whom should he meet across the table but the man who had bought his house? He got the work because it was much easier for the client to say 'yes' to my friend based upon the openness and integrity he had displayed in the earlier negotiation. You would be surprised how often this kind of 'coincidence' occurs. Often even those one-off transactions that appear to be isolated and transitory have consequences elsewhere.

In a culture of infinite choice and fierce competition, reputation and image become everything. Behaving ethically, enhancing trust, and building quality, lasting relationships is simply good for business. It can help to build a positive reputation, maintain staff loyalty as well as attract investment and custom. It helps to meet some of the increasing social expectations such as transparency, impact on the environment and employee needs. The methodology described here can also make the process of negotiation much more efficient financially and emotionally. This is why you need to become a skilled negotiator.

Negotiating from positions

The traditional approach to making agreements tends to be one of negotiating from a position. If I want to buy something from you, I will usually start with a very low offer and grudgingly increase it in small increments. I will tend to keep my cards to my chest and give away as little information as possible. On the other side, you will probably counter my low offer with something significantly higher and also give sparingly both in terms of price and information. We may agree somewhere in the middle or we may not reach agreement at all. There are a number of problems with this approach to negotiating.

Firstly, the starting position has nothing to do with the value of the product or service we are talking about. My opening offer could be completely arbitrary just to get the process started but is more likely to be related to what I would like to pay or what I can get away with.

The other problem with this approach is that when we state a position, and we don't achieve it, it may look and feel like failure or loss of face. In this way our ego can often get entangled with positions and the process then becomes a battle of wills where more for you means less for me.

Additionally, this process of bargaining from positions does not always produce an agreement. Even if it does, it may not be the best solution, as this approach does not provide an environment where the most creative options are generated.

Negotiating in this way is also exhausting and

inefficient: exhausting because it can be quite confrontational; inefficient because we can often dig into positions for long periods of time without making any progress.

During the 2003/04 firemen's strike the union's demands centred on a £30,000 basic salary. This appeared on banners at every picket line, the firemen became quickly identified with this position, and acceptance of anything less would look like a climbdown by the union. Much of the employers' energy was spent attacking this position by giving reasons why it was not a reasonable demand. The position took the focus away from dealing with the substance of the real underlying concerns and talks broke down a number of times, creating a long and painful dispute for the firemen, the employers and the public.

What is a good agreement?

Most people take a positional stance to making agreements because they don't realise there is another way. Positional bargaining can be an intimidating process which can lead to being either confrontational or passive. If someone takes a confrontational or 'hard' approach, they will give as little as possible while trying to gain as many concessions as possible from the other party. They see the negotiation options as either winning or losing and their priority tends to be winning. Those who take a passive or 'soft' approach want to avoid confrontation at all costs, so will often 'give away' whatever it takes to pacify the other party. Their priority tends to be managing the relationship.

Often of course, people take a middle path and come to a compromise somewhere between the two. Compromising between the positions still does not address the issue of interests and value and does not always provide the wisest solution. The classic example is that of the two sisters who argued over an orange: they both wanted the whole fruit. Because they could not agree, the mother decided for them by cutting the orange in two and giving one half to each sister. One sister ate the fruit and threw away the peel while the other used the peel for cooking and threw away the fruit. Clearly an agreement was reached through compromise, but it did not satisfy the needs of the two parties involved. Neither was the outcome efficient, as there was waste: half the peel and half the edible fruit was thrown away.

Efficiency in negotiations includes not leaving anything on the table. A much more elegant solution would have served the interests of each girl and nothing would have gone to waste. Also positional bargaining can be exhausting and time-consuming. Behaviour tends to breed behaviour and often a hard negotiator will get a similarly hard response from the other party simply because the other party feels they need to protect their own interests and not be trampled on. This can lead to a confrontational clash of wills producing an environment that stifles creativity and co-operation.

Positional bargaining does nothing to cultivate lasting relationships as people may leave feeling battle-weary rather than having reached a wise agreement.

This is unlikely to result in either party feeling comfortable enough to come back at some point in the future. Often in such a climate, people give little attention to implementation planning and find that there are problems in the detail or are left with the impression at some later stage that they could have done better.

So, an agreement is a good one if it satisfies the following:

- The interests of each party are satisfied where possible.
- The solution is the best possible from the options identified — there is no waste.
- The agreement is reached efficiently.
- It is possible and practical to implement the agreement.
- The agreement stands the test of time.
- The relationship is managed in a positive and constructive way.

Often positional bargainers will have a high concern for satisfying their own interests and a low concern for yours. It is worth establishing the style of the other party as soon as you can, during or even before the negotiation, as this will tell you much about their approach to you.

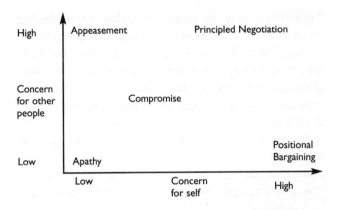

Determining the other party's approach will allow you to skilfully plan your strategy. If you are dealing with hard positional bargainers there are a number of things you can do to move them a little further up the scale that demonstrates concern for your interests. In the next section we will describe techniques that will help to bring the whole process of negotiation much more within your control.

What's your style?

Imagine you are one of 20 strangers sitting in a room. You are each sitting across from somebody on the other side of the table and somebody comes into the room and makes you an unusual offer. They say that they will give ten thousand pounds each to the first two people that can persuade the person opposite to stand, come around the table and then stand behind their chair. What would you do? Think carefully about your answer to this question for a minute and it will give you an idea as to how you approach any process of agreement.

While you are thinking about it, complete the following simple questionnaire about your approach to negotiations, which has been adapted from Fisher and Ury's book on this subject, *Getting to Yes*.

a. Other party are friends.
b. Other party are adversaries.

a. The goal is agreement.
b. The goal is victory.

a. Make concessions to cultivate the friendship.
b. Demand concessions as a condition of the relationship.

a. Be soft on the people and the problem.
b. Be hard on the problem and the people.

a. Trust others.
b. Distrust others.

a. Change your position easily.
b. Dig in to your position.

a. Make offers.
b. Make threats.

a. Disclose your bottom line.
b. Mislead as to your bottom line.

a. Accept one-sided losses to reach agreement.
b. Demand one-sided gains as the price of agreement.

a. Search for the single answer: the one *they* will accept.
b. Search for the single answer: the one *you* will accept.

a. Insist on agreement.
b. Insist on your position.

a. Try to avoid a contest of will.
b. Try to win a contest of will.

a. Yield to pressure.
b. Apply pressure.

Number of a's: ☐   Number of b's: ☐

If you scored a high number of a's, this probably means that you take a co-operative approach to making agreements. You will probably have a passive style and tend to avoid conflict wherever possible; even compromising your own needs in the interest of smoothing the relationship and getting some kind of agreement.

In the question I asked above, regarding the offer of £10,000, there could be a couple of possible responses; perhaps you avoided engaging in the game at all because you don't like situations where there are winners and losers. You would not like to have been seen as silly by jumping up and running around to the other side of the table and perhaps suspected the whole thing was a bit of a trick. You would rather avoid involvement and prefer to pass responsibility for getting to a solution to the other party sitting across from you. Alternatively it may be that you would have leapt up from your chair and run around to the other side before anything was agreed with your partner. This demonstrates a style that resolves conflict by trying to solve the other party's problems. This would put you in the position where they got the ten thousand pounds and you relied on their goodwill to share something with you. Negotiators that exhibit this style make attempts to maintain relationships with the other party, smooth over conflicts, downplay differences, and are most concerned with satisfying the needs of the other party.

If you scored a high number of b's, this probably means that you take a much more competitive approach to making agreements. You will probably have a strong assertive style, are willing to take risks and, above all, like to win. In looking for a solution to the offer made in the above scenario you may have shouted at the person opposite you to run around and come behind your chair, promising to share the money with them afterwards. This would put you in the position of controlling the process and how the money was shared out. Did you consider telling a little white lie and saying that you wouldn't be able to move because you were carrying a bit of an injury? This kind of approach is within the capability of the competitive negotiator because they are more concerned about getting results than managing the relationship. Negotiators who exhibit this style are results-oriented, self-confident, assertive, are focused primarily on the bottom line, have a tendency to impose their views upon the other party, and in the extreme can become aggressive and domineering.

If your score was balanced between a's and b's then you probably tend towards compromises in your approach to making agreements. Your style is most likely to favour some form of agreement that is equitable for each party involved on all issues under discussion. In the exercise above, you probably went for the obvious solution of offering to split the ten thousand 50/50 with your counterpart across the table as long as one of you moved fast. Would you have been caught up in who was going to move first? When it came down to it, you would probably have done the running yourself as those who tend towards compromising will favour managing the relationship over absolute results. Negotiators who exhibit this style aim to find the middle ground, often split the difference between positions, frequently engage in give-and-take tradeoffs, and accept moderate satisfaction of both parties' needs.

The other, perhaps less obvious approach, which really lies outside the analysis of our simple questionnaire, is the principled approach that we are asserting here. It is one where you both see yourselves as joint problem-solvers and come up with the most imaginative solutions. In the exercise with the strangers and the offer of ten thousand pounds, if you were to stand up and suggest that you both get behind each other's chairs then you could be in for ten thousand pounds each. If you look carefully at the way the offer is worded, there is scope for that kind of agreement if you are looking for it. Instead of focusing your efforts on how to best split the ten thousand, you could both end up with the full amount. This means looking beyond the obvious and identifying joint solutions to problems in a creative way. Negotiators who demonstrate this collaborative approach use open and honest communication, focus on finding creative solutions that mutually satisfy both parties, are open to exploring new and novel solutions, and suggest many alternatives for consideration.

The truth is that you probably use many of these differing styles under different circumstances, but what this exercise will help to identify is the underlying style that you tend to feel most comfortable with. The material in this book is designed to help you build upon your natural attributes and be as much yourself as possible by applying some useful tools and techniques. This allows you to recognise where and when the most effective styles are applied and perhaps strengthen those techniques in the areas that will give you the most beneficial results. Consider repeating the questionnaire again once you have finished reading this book. This will allow you to judge whether your attitude to making agreements has changed.

Negotiating with integrity

Negotiating with integrity is a different approach altogether to bargaining from either hard or soft positions. If integrity is about wholeness, when we negotiate with integrity we attempt to see the bigger picture. It is about understanding and satisfying our own needs, but it is also about understanding and satisfying the other party's needs and doing this in a way that is both fair and efficient. It is also driven by the agreements we make being easy to implement and durable and by our awareness of their impact on all parties. And it is worth doing this because it works. As mentioned earlier, this is not a question of acting with integrity out of some moral obligation or sense of righteousness. You are more likely to be successful at making agreements if you are clear about the other party's as well as your own needs and you set about deliberately satisfying them both. This process is much more likely to give you the best solution that will stand the test of time and also allow you to maintain a relationship with those you are negotiating with.

I put the issue of behaving with integrity right at the front of this book because it is a thread that runs through all of the material. Of course, everybody sets the bar at a different height when it comes to personal ethics and it is not my intention to dictate those standards. When I run workshops on the subject of negotiating with integrity, I find it much more powerful to ask some of the difficult questions regarding this topic and allow others to answer for themselves.

We all need to be able to determine our own code of conduct and be able to explain and, if necessary, defend our behaviour to ourselves, compared to the standards we set. It seems that there is always a cost associated with where we decide those standards are. If we set our standards high, there may be an associated material cost.

For example, when I worked for a corporate organisation, the construction standards for building new plants were set at a level consistent with those of the country with the highest technical standard where the company had a presence. In other words, if the company had a factory in Germany, which perhaps had the highest technical specifications, then if the same factory was built in rural India, the German specifications would be used even if local legislation allowed for less exacting standards. Even though there was a financial implication to this, the company's interests of integrity and consistency regarding environmental and safety standards were reflected in the policy.

If you set your standards low, then it may be your reputation that suffers and as a result you have difficulty getting people to trust you in the future. If it is the other party that behaves with questionable integrity, then you may pay a price in terms of time and effort as you ensure you challenge, probe and confirm that you are getting the best deal possible.

In determining your own personal ethical standards it will be interesting to reflect on the values and beliefs exercises in later chapters. Is integrity included in your list of core values? Do your beliefs about success and money influence your personal success in negotiations? Is there a belief there for example, that those people you know who have been successful really achieved it through dishonesty or deception?

The answer to some of these questions will help you to identify any patterns in your behaviour to do with past agreements and determine your attitude to the process of negotiation that you inevitably take with you in the future. Understanding some of these fundamental drivers will help you to pinpoint your own style and code of ethics and establish whether making adjustments will bring you better results.

It is important to understand that those you negotiate with will probably have different levels of integrity compared to yours. This means that you need to be constantly on your guard and if you feel that the other party is willing to put your interests at risk, then using some of the tools and techniques described in this book will help you to protect yourself. My personal take on the matter of integrity is to aim for the highest standards you possibly can. In my experience, not only does it yield excellent results at the negotiation table, it is also good for mental and emotional health. There is something fundamentally satisfying about demonstrating consistency between our values, words and actions and conversely, something inherently stressful if our personal ethics allow us to deliberately take advantage of other people, regardless of the gains we feel we make as a result. Consider also that we most often slide down, rather than up, the scale of integrity during the heat of negotiations. I therefore find it important to have identified a personal standard and maintain that rather than being drawn into playing the other party's game.

To really make this system work we need to consider and actively manage both the people and the process.

Managing the process

There are a number of key principles that can be used to manage the process of reaching agreements. They include techniques to identify underlying interests, generating creative options, as well as practicalities such as managing the environment and energy. These principles fit alongside some of the people-management issues to provide a framework for approaching any negotiation.

> • **Be clear about what you want**. This is often not as obvious as we think. By taking positions in a negotiation we can often obscure our real, underlying interests and get locked into arguing for a position that may be only one way of satisfying our needs.

- **Be clear about what the other side wants**. This is about identifying the other party's underlying needs. I describe this process as identifying values and interests, and once they are understood, you can then start to 'expand the pie' and generate options that will aim to satisfy those needs. Understanding what the other party wants doesn't mean that you agree with it or think that it is reasonable. However, once you have identified it, whatever it is, you can deal with it. These skills include effective questioning, clarifying, summarising and option generation.

- **Stay divergent for as long as possible and generate creative options**. Very often negotiators will look for the single solution that will provide agreement as early as possible. Finding this single solution can be difficult particularly in complex negotiations that perhaps involve many parties. Time spent understanding values, followed by a stage in the process whereby options are generated in an attempt to satisfy those values, is much more likely to provide creative options. This means staying open for as long as possible before then converging on the solution or a combination that will satisfy both parties. This does not necessarily come naturally as we are taught to satisfy our own needs as quickly as possible. It will therefore require effort, awareness and discipline.

- **Focus on solutions, not problems**. Generally in life, whatever you focus on grows. Rather than giving your attention to the barriers to agreement, be constantly focusing on the options that will provide solutions to the issues. Rather than asking what is wrong, ask what it would take for us to reach agreement. This skilful use of language and particularly the use of questions is a key skill in the armoury of the effective negotiator. Often by asking a different question you will get a completely different shift in the focus of a negotiation. Again, we are often taught to focus upon the things that are causing us problems rather than those things that will provide answers. The shift in emphasis will require conscious effort. The power of questions and how they can affect the outcomes you get is discussed in the chapter on communication.

- **Use objective standards**. Once you have identified mutual interests and it comes down to agreeing the money, the square metres, the length of the lease, or whatever the substance of the negotiation is, then it is important that some independent reference point is used. This may be market value, list price or expert opinion. Rather than agreeing in response to the power or pressure exerted by the other party, agree only on the basis of some objective criteria. As Sir Winston Churchill said, 'Never yield to pressure.'

- **Plan for the negotiation**. As with war and decorating, in negotiations, preparation is everything. We will provide a framework at the end that will allow you to enter a negotiation having prepared as fully as you possibly can. This refers not only to the planning before a negotiation, but also to the planning that follows. Often, negotiators succeed in the negotiation room only to meet unanticipated difficulties at the implementation stage.

Managing the people

Although they are intimately linked, we need to make a distinction between the human factors and the issues of substance in the negotiation. If we confuse these two, we can often attack the people when we need to attack the problem.

Because human beings are unpredictable creatures we need to manage things such as emotions, needs and perceptions. Dealing with these first will allow us to tackle the challenge of making an agreement as joint problem-solvers rather than adversaries. However, this is not about being nice; I can understand your position, I can listen empathetically and I can get a good idea of the pressures you are under but that should not affect the selling-price of the house, the hourly rate or the pounds per square metre that I end up paying. Just because I understand you, does not mean that I agree with you. So, an important step is to separate the people and the issues.

Managing the people should start with you understanding yourself a little more clearly. Then you need to understand the other side and find out how your relationship can bring benefits to you both. The following is a brief outline of some of the principles and skills that we will discuss in a little more detail regarding managing people.

- **Raise your standards**. If you go into a negotiation with low expectations, you will get poor results. This system is designed for you to increase your chances of getting it all: satisfying your needs, the other party's and also managing the relationship so that you can effectively do business in the future.

- **Develop an attitude of abundance**. One of the keys to making this system work is the understanding that people see the world not as it is, but rather how they think it is. This means that we need a good understanding of how people filter their experiences through the lens of their beliefs about themselves and life. Your attitude as you enter a negotiation is often to do with your beliefs and will impact on the outcome of your negotiations more than anything else. For example, many people see the world as a place of limited resources and therefore the more that you get, the less there is available for me. Now, on one level this may be true. Take the availability of oil for example, which is dwindling. However, the underlying interest in this resource is about the utilisation of available energy. If we understand this underlying interest, then we can expand the pie and include other energy sources which are much less limited; things such as wave power and wind power can be included which are in much more abundant supply. This is a simplification of a complex area, but illustrates the point that if we reframe and expand the point of focus we can create much more imaginative solutions. So, if you enter a negotiation with an attitude of scarcity, then all you will do is crank up the pressure to make agreements that don't meet your highest expectations. We will look at beliefs and perceptions in more detail later on.

- **Be co-operative, rather than competitive**. If the best negotiations really do satisfy the needs of both parties, then you are more likely to reach a successful outcome if both parties see themselves as joint problem-solvers rather than competitors. The idea of competition is a product of the scarcity-consciousness we have described above. Often when you perceive things differently it is possible to find other ways of satisfying needs or expanding the pie.

- **Communicate**. To become an effective negotiator you need to become a master communicator. This not only means communication with the other side, but also communication with yourself. Understanding yourself is where you should start for all negotiations. I don't mean you should enter into long-term therapy to analyse your childhood; I do mean get clear about your needs, the other party's needs and develop the skills to get you through the negotiation in the most effective and efficient way possible.

The principles

Focus on Values and Interests, Not Positions

We've already described how, more often than not, people tend to approach negotiations with a position in mind. The negotiator can become ego identified with the position and shifting from this will be associated with giving something up, making concessions or losing face. Consider two women in a restaurant. They are arguing over whether the door should be open or closed. The waitress comes over and politely asks them both to explain their reasons. One wants the fresh air that would be provided by the door open, the other wants it closed to avoid the draught. The waitress thinks for a while and then opens a window at the back of the restaurant. This not only prevents a draught from reaching the diners but also provides fresh air. Both diners are satisfied with the outcome. Without understanding the values of each party it would have been very easy to get locked into a positional stance about whether the door should be open or closed.

The more we identify with a position, the harder it is to move and the more it takes attention from the real, underlying interests that we are trying to satisfy. Behind every position there is a value. If you want your kids to go to bed at 8.30, then that position reflects an interest that may be about getting some time on your own, instilling discipline or making sure your kids get enough sleep. 8.30 is the position you take, but the interests are the things you really want to satisfy. In the earlier example of the sisters and the orange it is clear that if an analysis of their values, or interests had been made, then a much more elegant solution could have been found. One sister would have taken the peel for cooking and the other sister the fruit for eating. This would have satisfied both parties and would have been an efficient and waste-free outcome. The key to effective negotiation lies in looking behind the positions and identifying the values and interests that need to be satisfied.

The things that people want to satisfy operate at a number of different levels. I've called them values and interests. Values are those core human needs such as security, achievement, health, creativity or freedom.

Interests are the things you wish to satisfy right now such as maximising the selling price, not sitting in a draught, getting a piece of orange peel as a cooking ingredient or getting the kids to bed on time. But notice that the interests are an extension of the values. You may wish to maximise the selling price to provide you with financial security or a sense of achievement; you may not want to sit in the draught because you value your health; you want the orange peel because cooking is the way that you satisfy your creative urges; you may be interested in getting the kids to bed on time because you value the freedom you get from the time on your own or with your partner. Your current interests are always attempting to satisfy something that you value. Understanding this relationship is a key first step in understanding your behaviour in negotiations. This holds true for you and for the other party.

Before you attempt to identify the other side's values you must first of all be clear about your own. This may not be as obvious as it seems as we often have multiple values that exist at a number of different levels. Values provide us with a feeling of right or wrong about things: they are deeply embedded in our unconscious thinking processes and were formed very early in our lives through our upbringing and other formative influences. These provide us with a general background attitude towards life and can be seen reflected in our behaviour. For example, if financial security is a primary value, you will attempt to satisfy this in the key areas of your life. This will be reflected through your actions and you will satisfy this desire for financial security before, and sometimes at the expense of, other values. So, you may do a job that is unfulfilling but secure if security is a stronger value than self-expression. Your feeling of satisfaction and contentment will be linked to the level of financial security you feel, not only in your professional life, but perhaps also in your personal life.

At a more immediate level, you will have particular interests to satisfy. These will be an out-flowing or an extension of the more core values we have just described. For example, you may have an interest in tidying your house because you value a clean and ordered environment. Notice that behaviour is driven by a need to satisfy these underlying interests and values. This relationship between our values, interests and behaviour is at the heart of making effective agreements.

Identify your values

Before attempting to identify the values and interests of the other party, it is important to be clear about your own. Values are those really fundamental things that give you a sense of right and wrong in life and need to somehow be satisfied otherwise a sense of lack will result. In one way or another we are forever trying to satisfy those values that we feel most strongly about. To identify your own values answer the following questions:

- What are the things that are most important to you?
- What are the things that have consistently driven your behaviour in life?
- What would you like to be remembered for?

Write down the answers to these questions and see if you can identify any patterns in your life. If you are still having trouble identifying your core values, have a look at the list below and choose the three things that you identify most strongly with. Make the list, then put them in priority order in terms of strength of preference. When you have your shortlist, test them against your behaviour. What do your actions over time tell you about your values? For example, if you are identifying adventure and freedom as your core values, yet you are in an unfulfilling job, working for somebody else, with little autonomy, then there are some values stronger than adventure and freedom driving you. It may be responsibility or it may be financial security. Identify what you are demonstrating consistently through your actions and you will have a good idea of the values that you are satisfying.

Achievement	Integrity
Adventure	Intimacy
Affection	Involvement
Comfort	Love
Competitiveness	Loyalty

Co-operation	Passion
Creativity	Personal Development
Fame	Pleasure
Family Happiness	Power
Freedom	Recognition
Friendship	Responsibility
Harmony	Security
Health	Success
Self-respect	Wealth
Spirituality	Wisdom

In order of priority, my three key values are:

1.

2.

3.

Once you have a prioritised list of values you will have a better insight into your more immediate interests. Every time you go into a negotiation you must be crystal clear about the things you are trying to satisfy. Surprisingly, most people are not clear and often approach the negotiation by being reactive to the other party's position.

People often say that they go into a negotiation having had the interests determined for them, for example, by your boss or company policy. It then becomes part of your job to ensure you have clearly elicited your boss's interests and helped him or her to look beyond any simple position they may impose. In this case, your first negotiation is with your boss. Your personal values and interests will still play a part in these circumstances. If your interests are in looking good to your boss then the absolute outcomes of the negotiation will be less of an interest to you than the way that your performance is perceived.

The power of identifying values and interests is that there is often more than one way they can be satisfied. As with the women in the restaurant, looking beyond positions and understanding the underlying needs may create a whole new world of possibilities for agreement.

Discover the other party's values

Identifying your own values and beliefs is one thing, but what about the party you are negotiating with? It may not be particularly straightforward to elicit the needs of those you are dealing with; there may be several parties involved and people usually have multiple interests; they may not be clear about these things themselves or they simply may not want to disclose them. Discovering the other party's interests can be done directly or indirectly. The direct approach is to ask them! Ask why they have chosen a particular position or what it is they are trying to satisfy. This approach may give you the information you are looking for and then allow you to start generating some options around satisfying those interests.

If they lack clarity or simply don't want to give information away, then there are a couple of methods that may help to gather information about the other party's relationships, motivating factors, values and interests. The first is putting yourself in their shoes and the second is the skilful use of questions. Let's look at each of these in a little more detail.

Put yourself in their shoes

It is said that Mahatma Gandhi's habit before he entered a negotiation was to put himself in the shoes of every party involved in the negotiation, as well as the position of an independent observer. He would ask himself, 'What is it they are interested in and what would satisfy those interests?' Putting yourself in the position of those you are trying to reach agreement with gives you a unique insight into their thinking and therefore the things that are motivating them.

Here's a simple visualisation exercise that you can undertake to help determine the interests of the other party.

1. Picture the person whom you are going to be in negotiation with. Imagine them sitting across from you in the negotiating room. Picture the room as clearly as you can and create the emotional and physical environment with as much detail as you are able.

2. Then see yourself float above the other person and 'sink into' their body. You are now in their shoes; look through their eyes and try to see the world from their perspective. From their viewpoint you can see your own body sitting across the table from them. What are they thinking and feeling about you? What are the things they are likely to be interested in satisfying and how can this familiar person sitting across from them help in the resolution of the thing you are trying to negotiate? What pressures are they likely to be under and what are they likely to be motivated by more than anything else?

3. Next float out of their body and above the table. Imagine that there is somebody that you admire and respect who is observing the process from a short distance. They may even be viewing the proceedings through one of those one-way mirrors that looks onto the room. It may be someone that you know, or it may be a role model whose wisdom and insight you admire. What would this independent observer be witnessing and how would they feel about the approach you are taking? If they had a piece of advice for you, what would it be?

4. Finally, float back into your own body and ask yourself if you now have a new insight into the values, interests and needs of the other party.

What would it take for them to say 'yes' today and what could you do or say to make that difference?

Once you have undertaken this exercise, complete the negotiation preparation sheet included in Chapter 6. People sometimes feel that having an insight into the other party's thinking creates emotions of sympathy and understanding which will weaken their own position. It is important to remember that understanding where the other party is coming from is not the same as agreeing with them. Having this understanding will significantly increase the chances, not only of your developing a strategy that will take their needs into account, but also of your reaching agreement quickly and efficiently.

The power of questions

The skilful use of questions is one of the simplest and most powerful ways of eliciting the values, interests and perceptions of the other party. Questions will allow you to gather important information as well as help to build the relationship with the other party by demonstrating understanding and empathy. Asking the right questions at the right times can completely change the focus and direction of a discussion and provide breakthroughs where they did not exist before. In our communication we are often driven by the desire to have our own point of view understood. This can lead us to be very one-sided in our communication, listening ineffectively to what the other party is telling us and perhaps being dogmatic in emphasising our own interests. If the other party is taking the same approach, then communication may not happen at all. When you actively seek understanding by asking questions, you will get a very different response from the other party. Skilfully crafting questions is part of the art of good negotiation.

There are a number of categories of question, each of which can be used in a different way:

- Non-directive questions
- Directive questions
- Empowering questions
- Disempowering questions
- Possibility questions

Non-directive questions are open questions; in other words, they cannot be answered with a simple 'yes' or 'no', and they are a good way of encouraging the expression of feelings or opinions. For example, asking 'How do you feel about this particular option?' or 'What is it about this proposal that you object to?' rather than 'Are you unhappy with the proposal?' will give you a lot of information about the things that are of value to the other party. Such questions tend to draw out the other side and increase the chances of them revealing their real concerns. Non-directive questions can help to build trust and effective communication as they demonstrate an interest in the other party who will appreciate your willingness to discuss their point of view. It may also give them a sense of security and control as these questions give them an opportunity to present their case in their terms.

Directive questions ask for expansion or evaluation of a specific area. 'What are the areas that you are specifically concerned about?' or 'How exactly was it you arrived at that figure?' are directive questions focusing down on particular areas of interest. Directive questions are opportunities for focusing on solutions rather than problems as they allow you to direct attention towards the areas of agreement and away from the areas of disagreement, for example 'Under what circumstances would that proposal be acceptable to you?' or 'Do you see how this could be of particular benefit to you?' Directive questions can also help to move the other side towards accepting your proposal by highlighting the benefits to them.

Disempowering and Empowering Questions
The way that our thinking processes work means that you get certain kinds of answers to certain kinds of questions. For example, if you ask the other party 'Why can't we seem to work this out?' you will get a litany of reasons why not. If you ask yourself 'Why is this always such hard work?' your brain will immediately say 'Here's why ...' and start giving you a list of barriers to making the process easy. These tend to be **disempowering questions** because they

focus on the barriers to making progress. Asking these questions will often keep you in an endless pattern that will not provide any positive breakthrough. If you are constantly asking yourself 'Why me ...?' then there is very little possibility of finding a constructive way of taking you to the next level. 'Why do these things always happen to me?' 'Why do I never seem to be able to get the things that I really want?' are examples of disempowering, problem-focused questions.

Disempowering questions

- are problem-focused.
- create a cycle of blame.
- highlight the barriers to agreement and present the solutions as being out of our control.
- lead to defending positions, limit creativity and discourage action.

For example:

- Why does this always seem to happen to me?
- What if this doesn't work?
- Why is my boss always unfair?
- Why is this going wrong?
- Why is this so hard?

By asking different questions you can completely shift the focus from the problems to the solutions, for example 'What would it take for us to make a breakthrough right now?', 'What action could I take that would make a difference and make the process much easier?', 'How would I feel if we were able to solve this problem?' These are much more empowering questions. Empowering questions are not only solution- rather than problem-oriented, but also shift the sense of responsibility by focusing on what you can do regardless of the other party's plans.

Empowering questions

- are solution-focused.
- provide new understanding.
- give us a greater sense of responsibility.
- move us to taking action.

For example:

- What can I do right now that would make a difference?
- What would it take for us to move to the next level?
- How would it feel if we made a breakthrough now?
- How can I make this process easier, or more fun?
- What would I have to do to be financially secure for life?

- How much will this matter to me in five years time?
- What is really working at the moment?
- What would the best outcome look and feel like?
- How can I turn this experience to my advantage?

The questions you ask are an indicator of your point of focus. If you ask a different question, you change your reality by altering your point of focus.

For example, when somebody upsets you, what are the questions you ask?

Are they disempowering and reactive?

- How could she treat me this way?
- Why does this always seem to happen to me?
- How could they do this to me?

Or are they empowering and creative:

- I wonder why she is behaving like this?
- What else could this mean that I've not thought about?
- How can I best communicate my positive interests in this situation?

Questions will determine your point of focus. Your point of focus is simply the direction that you choose to take in your thinking and emotions. Disempowering questions will focus you upon the things that are going wrong and the barriers to making progress. Empowering questions focus you on finding solutions as well as engendering a sense of personal responsibility by getting you to think about the things that you can do to make a difference. Asking 'What can I change right now that will make a difference?' brings the focus back to the things that you can control. We mentioned Gandhi's success as a negotiator earlier; he was constantly asking 'How do we find a non-violent way of making progress?' The quality of the questions we ask can often provide us with the breakthroughs we desire. Notice that it is a matter of choice where you focus your thinking. Where you direct your attention is simply a habit you have learnt. Constantly looking to focus on solutions through the use of empowering questions will make a big difference in all your communication, not just your negotiations. Try this exercise right now:

Think of a challenge that you are currently facing in your life and ask yourself the following questions:

- What is it that is going wrong?
- Why does this seem to be such hard work?
- Does this kind of problem arise a lot for me?

Notice how you feel when you ask the questions and listen to your inner dialogue as you answer. Then ask yourself the following questions:

- How would it feel if I solved this problem right now?
- What could I do that would make a difference immediately?
- How have I successfully solved similar problems in the past?
- How could I make this better?

Do you notice that the empowering questions make you feel completely different about yourself, your ability to find a solution and also about the problem itself? They help you to focus on what you can do rather than the fact that you may be stuck.

In this section we are still trying to gain a greater understanding of the other party's values and interests: the things that drive them to behave the way that they do. Asking the right questions is probably the most effective tool you have for establishing this information. Constantly asking 'What is it the other party is trying to satisfy?' will help you to refine your understanding of the other party's interests. Asking 'What is it I am trying to satisfy?' will keep you focused on your key interests and stop you getting drawn into other less important issues.

Possibility questions are useful when generating options for agreement as they take you out of your normal range of thinking. They tend to start with 'What if ...?' and can open up a new perception of reality that you might not otherwise have considered.

Albert Einstein attributed his success more to his imagination than his rational thinking and famously started to develop his general theory of relativity when he asked himself a number of questions, including possibility questions. He sat looking at a clock and asked himself, 'How do we know what time it is?' then 'How do we see the clock?' His possibility questions were 'What if you could travel with the light?' and also 'What if you travelled faster than the light?' By asking himself some key questions he was able to reinvent a whole new reality that was outside the current thinking and perception.

If you observe conventional questioning you find that presuppositions built into our language often tend to contract our thinking rather than expand it. 'How come I never succeed?' presupposes not only that you don't succeed, but also that you never succeed. This is seldom true; it is simply a matter of focus. When I ask 'Really? Never? You never succeed?' you will agree that you do succeed, it is just your general perception that you don't. A person with this perception is simply blocking out the successes and choosing to focus on the failures. By asking a better question you may get a better answer. By asking 'What would it take for me to succeed?' or 'How would I know I've succeeded?' you immediately focus on finding solutions and identifying the things that you are trying to satisfy. 'How could they do this to me?' or 'How could he treat me this way?' presupposes that someone is deliberately doing something that is designed to harm you. This of course is all a matter of perception and may or may not be true. Asking instead 'I wonder what makes this person behave in this way?' immediately gives you a different perception of the other party's motives.

I choose to think that people have positive intentions, even if your perception is that their behaviour has a negative effect on you. This is particularly true in negotiations as people interpret a move as deliberately obstructive or even malicious. My experience is that the behaviour is much more likely to be about one party satisfying their own interests in the only way they currently see possible. Consider the example of when you are cut up in traffic. It is common to feel the rage build up and take the behaviour of the other driver as a personal attack. However, asking the question 'What is it that is going on in this person's life that is causing them to behave in this way?' may give you a number of different answers. They may be lost or confused about where to go, they may be desperately late for a meeting, on the way to the hospital or may simply be an inexperienced, unaware driver. There are any number of reasons that may cause people to behave in seemingly irrational ways but they will all be attempting to satisfy some interest that is positive for them. It is a matter of choice where you direct your attention. By asking better questions, you provide a new focus and change your perception of circumstances and behaviour. This is much more likely to provide you with opportunities to find solutions and make agreements.

While I was writing this chapter a friend of mine described an incident where he mediated a confrontation

45

between two sets of parents. One parent had been unhappy about how her child had been treated and had shouted aggressively at the child she thought was at fault. This was witnessed by the mother, who is the sister of my friend, and a confrontation ensued in the street. The confrontation escalated as the other parents got involved and my friend was called. His sister wanted him to support her stance, but instead of reacting to her request and taking sides, he asked himself a question: 'What was the intent of the first parent?' It was obviously to protect her own child and, although the communication had been handled badly in the heat of the moment, he could clearly see that each parent had a very positive interest they were seeking to satisfy. When he expressed this understanding he immediately got a much less defensive reaction from the aggressive mother. She agreed that the welfare of her child had been her primary concern and that she had not handled the intervention in the most constructive way. He also had to elicit agreement from his now very upset sister that she had exactly the same concern. Rather than be drawn into the confrontation he chose to help his sister understand her own interests, which were lost in the fog of emotions and aggression. This approach of asking a skilful question to identify the underlying interests provided the breakthrough to an amicable agreement.

Satisfy multiple interests

Being human beings we tend to have not just one interest we are trying to satisfy, but a number. When you are thinking of buying a car, you not only want one that fits the size of your family, you are also interested in fuel economy, condition and colour. There will be a hierarchy of needs in this case where some interests will be more important than others. You need to be clear about this prioritisation for yourself as well as trying to identify any multiple interests the other party may have.

A few years ago I was the contracts manager for a large engineering site and part of my responsibility was to negotiate the service contracts on behalf of all the site businesses. Rather than the local engineers negotiating rates for things like scaffolding and painting on an individual basis, I would do that on their behalf and secure better prices based upon larger volumes. In this case I had multiple interests to satisfy. Not only did I have an interest in the ongoing relationship with the service contractor, but I also needed to ensure that the local plant engineers trusted my judgement and felt I was getting the best deal on their behalf. In some ways, the performance of the contractor was of less importance to me than the perception of the businesses as they would have a greater impact on my chances of promotion. There may be circumstances where someone is seemingly focusing on price, delivery or size, when their real interest is in showing their boss how well they can perform.

In the case of negotiations within the European Union, each member state has dual interests to satisfy. Not only are they negotiating with the other states on things like membership, budgets and rebates, but they also have to go back to their individual countries and get the agreements accepted there. British Prime Minister Tony Blair was under considerable pressure from the other members of the EU to review a rebate agreement that was established more than 20 years ago. However, at home he was under even more pressure to maintain the agreement and would be considered weak if he gave anything away.

Consider that the other party may have a number of interests and unless these are taken into account then agreement may not be possible. When faced with a party that has multiple interests, it is a good idea to ask yourself if you could draft an agreement that would not only be acceptable to you, but would also meet all the other party's main interests. If you can't do that, then you are unlikely to reach agreement.

Ensure outcomes match values

The central point here is that the key to reaching agreement lies in ensuring that the outcomes satisfy your values as well as everyone else's. However, there is a difference between all parties getting what they like and their values being satisfied. For example, when you're involved in a property transaction, as the seller, you would like to maximise the price that you get; as the buyer, you would like to minimise what you pay. Neither party is going to get what they like, but the sale will occur if the values and interests are satisfied.

Recently my brother was buying a house and got into negotiation with the selling agent. The issue was the asking price of the house, but after some skilful questioning it became evident that the vendor's interests were about getting cash quickly as they were in financial difficulty. My brother's interest was in finding a place that was in a particular area, readily available and was in need of some renovation. All these conditions were met in this particular house. He had already sold his house so was able to produce the cash quickly. He was clearly in a position to satisfy the vendor's primary interest of a quick sale. The seller would like to have got more for his house, but both sets of values and interests were satisfied and the agreement was made.

It is easy to confuse satisfying interests with satisfying likes or preferences. This is about getting to the things that matter to both parties as quickly and efficiently as you can so that possible options for agreement can be identified.

Focus on values and interests, not positions: summary box

- Don't accept positions at face value; get behind them to determine underlying needs.
- Know your own drivers: your values and interests.
- Use questions skilfully to build understanding and trust and to establish the other party's values and interests.
- Everyone has multiple interests; be clear about your own and the other party's and which are most important.

Case study

Orchard Heights was a block of apartments comprising 25 units which, I had been informed by an agent friend, the owner was interested in selling. A consortium of investors was interested in buying, and they asked me to speak to the owner about his terms.

The elderly man who owned the block was hoping to retire in comfort and, although he was mentally and physically very alert, there seemed to be some hesitation about the sale. At our first meeting we had established a price for the apartments that he was happy with and that the investors were willing to match, so it seemed to me there was something else on his mind. He had not advertised the block anywhere and was very anxious that we should keep a low profile regarding the negotiations we were having. I was only too happy with this arrangement as I didn't want any competitors coming in at such an early stage of the negotiations. However, I had a couple of further meetings with him so that I could get to know him a little better and understand what might be making him hesitate about moving to the agreement stage.

I listened very carefully to him and asked him lots of questions. I eventually discovered that he had a son who was managing the block of apartments and he was worried about his son's employment prospects if the units were sold. The son was now in his forties and had never really made a success of any jobs he had undertaken. This included managing the apartment block: the units were never fully occupied and on occasions the father was incurring a loss. The vendor was worried that the new owner would get rid of his son, who would not be able to find more work; he would then be a continual burden during his father's retirement. He hadn't mentioned the possibility of the sale to his son for fear of being accused of deliberately putting him out of a job. This was why the owner was stalling.

I went away and thought about the options. I was acting as agent in this transaction and, as my fee depended upon it, my interest was clearly to get an agreement from both parties. The consortium of investors was keen to make the deal because the property fitted well with their investment strategy. The owner was ready to close if he could find a neat way of handling the delicate matter of his son.

After reviewing the options I made a proposal to the investors that would hopefully secure the purchase and keep everyone happy. Having discussed the options with them, I got the go-ahead from the investors and then went back to the owner with the proposal.

I suggested that we made the purchase at the agreed price and kept the son on as a 'consultant' or 'advisor' for a period of 18 months following the sale. This way the son would get a reasonable salary for the period as well as the status of consultant on his CV, which might help him secure another job in the future. He was pleased with the amount of work that he needed to do for the salary as it meant that he would have enough time to look for another position. The owner was happy as he had satisfied his interest of generating his retirement funds and he felt less like he was being disloyal to his son. The investors secured the property at the price they were willing to pay and considered the cost of the son's salary to be very small compared to the value of the purchase. The investment proved to be a good one, although I'm not sure if the son ever did get himself another job.

Analysis

Money isn't always the primary motivator in negotiations. The emotional factors always play a part and finding out people's real motives is not always easy. J.P. Morgan, the Wall Street tycoon, famously said, 'A man always has two reasons for the things he does — a good one and the real one.' People often have multiple interests that need satisfying. Only through building trust with the owner of the apartment block was I able to find the real barrier to agreement and consequently suggest a solution that satisfied all of his interests.

Also, when negotiations are conducted, there is often more than one party to satisfy. I was acting as agent between the investors and the seller and it was part of my job to understand and satisfy all of the potentially differing interests of the parties involved. Without understanding the underlying interests, it would have been easy to get locked into a positional bargaining situation over price when the real issues lay elsewhere. Having this understanding allowed me to expand the pie to include other less obvious solutions that in the end provided the keys to agreement.

2

Managing Perceptions

veryone sees the world through the filter of their perceptions. This includes you as well as the party you are negotiating with. The author Anaïs Nin said, 'We don't see things as they are, but rather as we are.' There is an ancient Sufi story about three blind men describing an elephant. The one who had felt the leg of the beast described the animal as being mighty and firm like a pillar. The one who had reached the ear described it as being large, broad and rough like a rug. The third blind man disputed the other descriptions. He had felt the trunk and said that the true description of an elephant was like a straight and hollow pipe, awful and destructive. Each had part of the information and all had perceived it differently. The key to breaking through to making agreements lies in understanding, managing and if necessary, influencing perceptions.

Understanding perceptions

Our perception of the world and other people is usually based upon our beliefs about things. One of the things we said earlier is that we need to raise our expectations going into any negotiation. The higher your expectations, the greater the likelihood that you will get a better result. However, if you have a belief that you are unworthy of great results in your life, or that everything in life is limited, then your attitude and behaviour cannot help but reflect these beliefs. If you believe you are negotiating over very limited resources then your option generation will also be limited and you may feel that more for the other side means less for you.

Beliefs are like commands to the nervous system and will be reflected in your thinking, language and behaviour. The trouble with beliefs is that we confuse them with the truth. Our beliefs are just one way of seeing the world, like the blind men and the elephant; they are not absolute truths, but only part of the story. We know this because there are many people who hold different beliefs about the same things in life. To communicate effectively with anybody and therefore increase your chances of making effective agreements, you will need to be clear about your own perceptions and also know something of the other party's too.

Have a look at the lists below and see if you can identify any obvious beliefs in your life that you carry into your negotiations.

Your empowering beliefs
- I am usually successful in the things that I try.
- I am worthy of success.
- People are usually motivated by positive intentions.
- I will usually find a way of making things work.
- We live in the most abundant of times.
- I am usually able to communicate my needs well.

Your disempowering beliefs
- I can never seem to get the things I really want.
- I am not clever/attractive/wealthy enough.
- Life is one problem after another.
- People are basically out only for themselves.
- You get rich by exploiting others.
- I'm not a person who can take risks.
- I'm not worthy.

As with your values, beliefs operate at a number of different levels. You will have global beliefs about life in general, things such as 'all men are ...', 'all women are ...', 'all rich people are ...' You will also have specific beliefs about yourself or particular people: 'I'm not clever enough', 'I can never seem to get the things I want ...' They also fall into the category of beliefs that empower you and those that limit you. Unfortunately, many of us have a long list of the latter and a shorter list of the former. Make a list of the things that form your view of the world.

This is relevant because it influences your expectations and therefore the standards you set for yourself before you enter any agreement-making process. This process of setting expectations is a key concept. In one sense you only get what you truly expect. Your expectations are based upon your beliefs about what you can achieve. To raise your expectations, and your results, change your beliefs about what you are worthy of achieving in your life.

Don't transfer your perceived fears onto the other party

Because we perceive the world in one way, we expect other people to see things the way we do. There is a story of a man breaking down in his car late at night. His mobile phone is dead and he is in a remote country location. Thinking he has passed a farmhouse some miles back, he starts to walk. As he walks he starts to think about his predicament and the likely reaction of whoever is in the house. 'It's late at night,' he thinks to himself, 'there's probably no-one up at this time.' When he reaches the farm, there is a light on in the hall. 'They've probably left it on over night,' he thinks. 'They will all be in bed and I'll have to get everyone up. In fact I'll probably have to bang on the door really hard so that they will hear me.' The story in his head starts to get worse. 'The farmer's probably been working all day and when he comes and realises I only want to use his phone, he will be furious.' By the time he reaches the door he is in a turmoil of agitation and as a result bangs on the door really hard. The door swings open almost immediately, 'Yes?' asks the startled farmer. The man blurts out, 'What do you mean acting like that? What kind of person are you? Can't you see I'm in trouble here?' He continues, wide eyed with anxiety. 'All I want is to use your phone, so don't even think about slamming the door on me ...' At which point the farmer slams the door.

We've probably all had some version of this happen to us where we almost predetermine the outcome by the attitude we go in with. There are a couple of key lessons from this story. One is that if our attitude does help to determine the outcome, then as we said earlier, going into a negotiation with positive expectations can help to give you better results. The second message is that often our internal story has nothing to do with the external reality. Recognising this can allow us to be a little more objective and open-minded in our approach. If we accept that our perceptions are limited as are the other party's, we are much more likely to work co-operatively in finding solutions and behave as joint problem-solvers rather than adversaries.

Their problem is your problem

If you truly are to see yourself as one part of a joint problem-solving team, then apportioning blame is not going to help either. Telling the other side that it is their fault, even if it is, may make you feel better, but is not the best approach to reaching a good solution. Be careful not to get caught in positions which require an acknowledgement that you are right; all that it will do is cause you to lose focus on your main objective which is to find a lasting agreement.

Where you are reliant upon agreement with this party, their problem is your problem. I remember travelling to a conference in a car once with a number of colleagues when we had a tyre blow-out. We pulled over safely and made preparations for changing the wheel as we were running a little late and all anxious to get to our destination. The owner of the car appeared from behind the boot and sheepishly announced that the spare wheel was being repaired and he had no replacement. In anger one of our team blurted out, 'Well, you do have a problem now, don't you?' It's easy to focus on the obstacles we have in front of us and label them as someone else's problem. It's harder, but much more effective to be joint problem-solvers and focus on the solutions by recognising we all have an interest in the outcome. There was a happy ending to the story as we managed to call the breakdown services and get to our conference, a little late, but in one piece.

In the change management book *Who Moved My Cheese?*, Spencer Johnson identified the approach that different people take when faced with challenging circumstances. When the characters depicted as rats found that what they were doing wasn't working, they changed their approach; the characters depicted as humans looked for someone else to blame. Identifying whose fault it is may make you feel a little better but it will not get you to an agreement faster. Break the cycle of your conditioning and look for solutions rather than problems.

When you know that someone has made a mistake try to keep your analysis of the situation specific and neutral. For example, we had a supplier who was consistently late with deliveries of key electrical components. This had caused us some costly down-time on a plant and we discussed the situation with the supplier concerned. We stated the problem in terms of symptoms; the cost of down-time and difficulty that our tradesmen were having in getting hold of particular components.

'We have lost 36 hours in the last week due to our feed pump breaking down. This has been due to lack of availability of the control valve. We just wanted your advice on how we could avoid that down-time in the future.'

The contractors knew very well that it was down to them and they responded by reviewing their supply systems as well as suggesting we hold certain comp-onents on site at their cost. We had experienced similar circumstances in the past and the approach had been to confront the contractors and push the problem directly at them. This led them to respond in a very defensive way and point out the shortcomings of our system. We were then locked into a spiral of blame, which got us no closer to finding a solution, but actually brought hostility into the relationship. By laying blame you entangle the substance of the problem with the people involved and risk not finding a suitable solution.

Influencing perceptions

The power to make agreements lies in managing perceptions. Advertisers understand this concept only too well and it is therefore important to understand some of the concepts used to influence and possibly manipulate your perceptions. The speed and complexity of our world and the way that our brains store information means that we tend to generalise and, when dealing with people, we form stereotypes. For example, once we learn how door handles work, we tend to generalise that information and approach all doors with a handle in the same way. If a handle on a door turns in the opposite direction to what we are used to, this is usually a surprise and we have to make adjustments in our brain and our body to cope. We tend to look for changes to this generalised store of information and often decisions are made based upon what we are able to compare it with. This is called perceptual contrast. For example, the salesman in a shop may show you the expensive suit first so that the next one will seem cheaper; if you'd been shown the cheaper suit first, that may have seemed too expensive. If you've just bought an expensive dress, paying £100 for a pair of matching shoes does not seem that expensive. What the sales people are doing here is reframing your perceptions.

Be aware that the reframing process is often used by positional bargainers. By setting an extreme price at the beginning of the bargaining process, they will look like they are making generous concessions if they bring the price down considerably. Go along and listen to a market trader sometime and you will see the concept in action.

> *'See this beautiful 50-piece bone china tea service? This will retail in the shop along the road for at least £200. But I'm not asking £200, I'm not even going to ask you for £100. Would it be worth paying £75, that's £125 less than you would pay in the shops? Probably, but I'm not even asking you for £75. Nor will I ask you for £50. I'm going to ask you for only £35, that's a massive saving of at least £165 ... Who'll give me £35 for this beautiful tea service and save themselves a fortune ...?'*

And on he goes. What he is doing is framing your expectations of the price by his opening suggestions. Of course his opening amount, or the other figures have nothing to do with the value of the tea service, but he focuses your attention on the massive reduction that he is making. This gives you the perception that you are getting a good deal and on the basis of that, he hopes you will buy. So often, positional bargainers will start high in the hope of influencing your perception of value.

There are a number of other psychological principles that influence our perceptions and it is worth understanding how they work so that you can be aware if they are being used to manage your behaviour.

- Scarcity
- Social reinforcement
- Social similarity
- Commitment
- Reciprocity

Scarcity

This also works if the things we want to purchase are perceived as being of limited availability, even if they have deliberately been made scarce. Items such as certain vehicles have a long delivery period to create the impression that they are in limited supply; or they may be advertised as a limited edition, which often creates a long waiting list. Studies in the United States found that juries do take evidence into account that has been deemed inadmissible by the judge. Simply because it has been denied to them, they want to use it. Anybody who has a teenage child will recognise how teenagers are attracted to the things that have been denied by their parents. Be aware that this scarcity consciousness can be deliberately cultivated and watch out for any links with core beliefs that you may have.

For example, many people in our culture have a belief that many of our resources are limited. Most of us value security in our lives and therefore to satisfy this value we may feel the need to get our hands on some of those limited resources. You can see this demonstrated during holiday periods such as Christmas when the supermarkets close for one or perhaps two days. Notice how many people embark upon a buying frenzy and stock up with food that would probably last for a month rather than a few days, simply because the availability has been denied them for a short time.

Sales people can make good use of this tendency, to force closure on a sale. For example, if you are negotiating the purchase of a used car, the salesman may make an offer, but then say 'It's only available at this price until the end of today.' This is clearly a tactic, but notice that it creates a sense of pressure to make a decision quickly. Stores often advertise a sale stating 'only while stocks last ...' All of these examples make use of the scarcity principle which taps into some of our most fundamental beliefs and values.

Social reinforcement

Often when we are not sure what to do, we are influenced by what other people do. Our market trader from the above example may have a couple of 'plants' in the audience who immediately take him up on his offer to buy his tea set. Because other people are rushing to buy, we often feel an impulse to follow. In a similar way the busker will always put a few coins in his or her tip jar so that people will think that others have already decided to give and that giving money is the right thing to do.

A few years ago there was a horrific murder in Central Park in New York that was carried out by a gang in full view of passers-by. There were plenty of witnesses around but none of the onlookers did anything to intervene because no-one else acted. If you do want help from a crowd of people, it is best to ask a specific person. Street entertainers do this very well as they will pick on an individual from the crowd to participate in the act. Even if that individual is reluctant, the entertainer will get support from the crowd, making it very difficult for the 'volunteer' to say no.

Social similarity

This social reinforcement is very powerful and particularly influential if we think that the people acting are similar to us. This feeling of similarity is one reason why getting into rapport with those you are negotiating with is so important. We will explain some of those skills in the next section. We tend to relate better and therefore like people who are socially similar to us, particularly if we think that they like us. These similarities are especially reinforced if the contact takes place in pleasant, positive circumstances. That is why a lot of influencing is done on the golf course, and why the party looking for the business will usually (deliberately) lose the game. The better you can help the guest feel, the stronger an unconscious connection is made between the positive experience and those with whom you are sharing the experience. This is why people at a make-up or jewellery party will usually buy something to please the hostess, who is usually a friend. It is also why the concept of good cop/bad cop works. The suspect is much more likely to confess to the good cop because there is some social similarity and liking implied.

Commitment

When people make a commitment to something of their own free will, then their behaviour is usually consistent with that commitment. This is particularly true if the commitment has been made in public. If someone in a public place asks you to keep an eye on their belongings while they nip to the toilet and you have agreed, notice that you feel a sense of responsibility to follow this through and the commitment feels even stronger if others around you have witnessed the exchange. It has been found that juries find it much more difficult to change their verdict if it has been indicated by a show of hands in front of the other jurors rather than by an anonymous ballot. During negotiations, watch out for people trying to get you to commit to things that you may not be ready for, particularly if it is in front of a group.

Reciprocity

People tend to feel a sense of obligation to repay another party even if whatever has been given was done so without any expectation. This is socially important as even if no strings were attached, if the recipient continues to receive without giving back in some way then that person will eventually be disliked. There is a story about Benjamin Franklin whereby he would use a technique of asking the other party if he could borrow a particular book. This would break the formal barriers separating the two, flatter the other person and also give them a comfortable feeling that the US president owed them a favour. There is often an issue around gifts, gratuities and entertainment between parties who are negotiating business. There is definitely a place for building relationships before agreements are made, as described below, but be aware that this can be contrived to make you feel as though you need to repay any generosity. It may be better to leave the informal activities until after the agreements have been made.

Building relationships

The more quickly you can build a constructive relationship with the person you are negotiating with, the better. It is easy to attribute sinister and destructive intent to some nameless, faceless entity, but very difficult once you meet the person face to face. The sooner you can get to know somebody and the more you find out about their communication style, preferences and social background, the easier it will be to manage the flow of communication. By developing a more comfortable emotional environment you will make it easier to break tense moments with a joke or some other informal comment. Make the effort to develop these relationships before you get into the negotiation room; arrive earlier and stay later so that you get the opportunity to influence their perceptions of you and also build this working relationship.

Be firm but flexible

So, what is a belief anyway? A belief is a feeling of certainty that something is right. You can see from some of the above examples that our perceptions of the world are influenced by a great number of things and are therefore not fixed. This is highly relevant to any negotiation process as you will arrive at the table with a set of perceptions and so will the other party.

Major breakthroughs in understanding often result from a change in beliefs, or a shift of perception. This is because the problem is one of perception rather than one in external reality. This is not a suggestion to see everything from the other person's point of view; it is to recognise that your perception is only one of perhaps many.

Parties lock into positions because they each think they are right. We constantly see this demonstrated in areas as diverse as marriage and international relations. Partners fight and nations go to war because one party feels they are right and the other wrong. All this does is to lock you into a bargaining position, making it harder to shift from this position and find other ways of reaching agreement. Once you focus on the values you are trying to satisfy, you are able to be firm but flexible when you enter any negotiation. You can be firm about those interests that do need to be met, but flexible about how that is achieved. This helps you to avoid taking a positional stance and leaves room for option generation. For example, when sending your kids to bed your interests may be to do with having time to yourself, instilling discipline and making sure they get enough sleep. Your kids' interests may be to do with fitting in with friends and not going to bed too early as well as developing some autonomy. Rather than digging into an absolute time of say 8.30, it may be agreed that they are in their room by 8.30, have time to themselves for half and hour and then lights are out by 9.00. This way the values of both parties have been discussed, understood and to the extent possible, satisfied.

Just to be clear, this is not about conceding to the other party's beliefs at the expense of your own. A course that people tend to take in relationships is making concessions, as they feel this will avoid confrontation and provide a better chance of agreement. When we make concessions in response to pressure alone, then we are rewarding abusive behaviour. I had a friend whose relationship was the most important thing in her life. As a result, she conceded on nearly every important area with her partner, just to keep the peace; she gave up her friends, hobbies and other interests. In the end, the man left her. Rewarding abusive behaviour demonstrates to the other party that abuse gets results. Any relationship is a dynamic interaction of understanding and communicating perceptions and satisfying needs. It is this dynamic that keeps the relationship alive. No relationship, whether personal or professional, is without conflict and this is not necessarily a bad thing. In fact relationships with no apparent conflict are often much less healthy than those with frequent conflict. It is how the conflicts are resolved that is the critical factor. Conflicts are events that can strengthen or deepen the relationship; they can create greater understanding, closeness and respect. If managed badly, conflicts can be extremely destructive, creating hostility, resentment and divorce.

In all relationships we get the best results if we are flexible enough to see things from the other party's point of view, but firm enough to ensure that the interests that are important to us are satisfied.

Discuss each other's perceptions

The best way to deal with these different perceptions is to get them out in the open and discuss them. What we are trying to do here is make a distinction between the problem you are trying to solve and the people on the other side of the table. We've already implied that on one level the people are the problem — or the person's perception of the problem, but this means it is all the more important to make the distinction. What is required is to address the people issue before you address the substance of the problem you are trying to solve.

You must acknowledge people's perception of the problem before you can make progress, regardless of whether you agree with their stance or not. Even if it is not important to you, it is obviously important to them, therefore it needs dealing with. Directly or indirectly signalling that the other party's perceptions are not important is tantamount to saying, they themselves are not important. You are very unlikely to make any lasting agreements with that kind of relationship.

We've already said that there is usually a positive intention behind most people's behaviour, even if you don't understand or agree with it. From their perspective, they are usually trying to improve a situation that is beneficial to them, and their behaviour and any position they take will be consistent with this. Ask yourself what beneficial intention from their point of view is behind the behaviour you are observing. This will help you to get more clearly into their shoes, or as the Native Americans say, 'Walking a mile in their moccasins.'

As with values, the starting point is to use questions as the key to getting an idea of the other side's beliefs. For example:

- How do you see the relationship between these two parties?
- What do you think are the key areas we need to discuss?
- This is my understanding of the situation ... how do you see it?
- What's your perception of ...?

For any of this to happen effectively, you will have to have taken responsibility for creating an environment where there is enough trust and openness for this kind of discussion to take place. Creating this environment will be the topic of discussion in the next section, which is on communication.

Notice that all of the skills that we have talked about up to this point are about laying the foundations for the negotiation to take place. We have been taking time to understand the other party; their values, interests and perceptions. Be clear that at this stage of the process you are information-gathering;

you are not looking for solutions. If you are comfortable enough with the other party, then often making
the process explicit and labelling the stages can be
helpful.

Managing perceptions: summary box

- Understand that perception is not reality, only
  one version; for you and for the other party.
- Understand the beliefs that shape your perceptions and ask yourself if they give you the best
  outcomes.
- Actively manage perceptions as part of the
  process, both yours and the other party's and if
  necessary, talk about them.
- Behave like joint problem-solvers not adversaries.
- Be aware how your perceptions can be
  influenced and never yield to manipulation or
  pressure, only to reason.

Case study

The lease was due to be renewed on an apartment in East London, where the current tenants had been living since it was built, just two years previously. Much of East London is undergoing huge development in preparation for the London 2012 Olympic Games, so there is plenty of building work but much of the infrastructure in terms of transport links is not yet complete. Because of rising management costs and interest rates the landlord needed to increase the rent. However, because the tenants had been incumbent for a couple of years and were willing to stay in spite of the less than ideal local environment, they wanted the rent fixed. The current lease expired at the end of the month after I was contacted, so both parties were under pressure to agree the terms of the renewal.

The landlord was a little nervous. There is an enormous amount of construction in the area as developers build apartment blocks to capitalise on the inevitable growth in the build-up to the Olympics. As a result of so many new apartments being built, landlords are facing fierce competition for tenants and many of the bigger developers are deliberately undercutting the smaller private investors in order to let their own properties. Since the announcement that the Olympics will come to London, property in this district has risen in value and there are huge plans to improve the whole area: new road, rail and canal links will contribute to a massive transformation. However, there will also be massive disruption; commercial buildings have been subject to compulsory purchase orders and knocked down to make way for new stadiums, competition venues and athlete accommodation.

The landlord of the flat knew that his tenants would have a wide choice of accommodation, and also that the area was not at its best because of the extensive development work. However, he also knew that, within a few years, after all the planned developments, the area would be highly desirable and the property would be worth significantly more both in terms of capital and rental value. The next two years were critical for his investment strategy to work.

From the landlord's point of view, he wanted to increase the rent in order to cover the increasing costs of maintaining and managing the apartment. He was also very keen to get the current tenants signed up for at least another year as he would incur high agent's fees if he had to source new tenants. He felt he had a reasonable relationship with the young couple renting the apartment, although on his last visit he had noticed that there were some signs of wear and tear; he wasn't sure how well they were treating the place. However, apart from a few late payments early in the tenancy, they usually paid their rent on time each month.

The tenants wanted to fix the rent at the current level if they could, but after their last conversation with the landlord, they had a feeling he might be angling for an increase. They were sure they had some valid arguments to support their case as the area was still being developed and the transport links were still not fully operational. Also, in their opinion the apartment was starting to look as though it could do with a lick of paint even though it was only a couple of years old. However, they did know what a hassle it would be to move and even though they would probably have had plenty of local choice, this flat was just on the canal, which they really liked, and they now had some friends in the development whom they saw on a regular basis.

Moreover, one of the tenants had started his own business in the previous year and was working from home. A move to another location would have meant changing telephone numbers and addresses on letter-heads as well as informing clients of the change. They really wanted to stay put, but could ill afford a hefty increase in rent. They thought the landlord was pretty reasonable but they didn't see him that much; he really only ever came if they called him with a problem.

When this negotiation started, the two parties made their initial demands through the lens of what they perceived their strengths to be rather than actually focusing on their real interests. The tenants insisted that the rent should remain at its present level because they could possibly have done better somewhere else, the flat was looking a little shoddy and they had been good tenants for the last two years. They claimed the area was like a building site and they ended by threatening to move somewhere else if their demands weren't met. The landlord on the other hand was arguing that he had fixed the rent for the last two years without increase and that the area was improving all the time. If the apartment was looking shoddy it was because they had been living in it and he reminded them that they had made some late payments early in the tenancy. They remained in deadlock for a while as they both dug into their respective positions.

This was broken when one of the tenants took the risk of declaring their interests:

'Look, we would prefer not to move out if the truth were told. We would prefer to stay here, but we are worried about paying for an increase in rent.'

Once the pattern was broken, they were able to discuss things a little more openly and talk about interests and values rather than make demands from positions. In the end they all agreed to sign up for another two years with an increase in two stages: a small rise at the start of the new tenancy for one year with a further increase in year two. The initial increase just met the landlord's need to cover his additional costs regarding interest rates and management fees, but didn't take into account all of his potential maintenance costs. In return for the smaller increase the tenants agreed to paint the apartment themselves, saving the landlord the cost of painting as well as the agent's fees for finding a new tenant. The tenants were happy that they had some security for the next two years and the landlord knew that the apartment would be occupied during his financially critical period.

Analysis
Perception is everything in negotiations. Notice that both the tenants and the landlord were looking at exactly the same things from a different point of view.

The tenants saw the rent as being high already in relation to what they felt they might pay elsewhere; the landlord thought it was legitimate to raise the rent since it had been fixed for two years. The tenants saw the landlord as being distant and uncaring; he felt he was being considerate by allowing them their privacy. They saw the apartment as being slightly run-down; the landlord saw the tenants themselves as the cause of the dilapidation.

When each party looked at the problem with their own perceptions, they spent their energy attacking the other's position and defending their own. They began to project their own fears onto the other party: the landlord's fears were that he wouldn't be able to make his financial strategy work whereas the tenants were more concerned about their living environment. Again, although the money was a central issue in the negotiation, the emotional element was playing a significant role, particularly as far as the tenants were concerned.

Notice also that this focus upon positions did nothing to satisfy their underlying interests. In fact by threatening to move somewhere else if their demands were not met, what the tenants were proposing was actually totally opposed to what they really wanted. It was only when real interests were declared that the negotiation could start properly. There is often a risk in declaring interests as we may feel that it makes us vulnerable to attack from the other party. However, if the other party is negotiating with you, it is likely that they need to satisfy needs of their own through you. One of the parties must take that calculated risk.

There is a story about the buy-out of the American publishing house Harcourt Brace Jovanovich (HBJ) by the large conglomerate General Cinema. HBJ was close to financial collapse and General Cinema was looking for a presence in the publishing industry. They felt that HBJ would be the perfect fit. When the two parties met across the negotiating table, HBJ was represented by Peter Jovanovich, the son of one of the company's founders, who obviously had a strong emotional investment in the survival of the family business. General Cinema was represented by Dick Smith, an aggressive entrepreneur who ran the company.

They all wanted the deal to go ahead and were each surrounded by advisors and primed for a tense and guarded negotiation. As Smith started to speak, Jovanovich interrupted the entrepreneur and the room bristled with anticipation at this deviation from the script. Jovanovich reached into his pocket and pulled out a small box, which he placed on the table between him and Dick Smith. He opened the box. Inside was an engraved HBJ watch that he pushed over towards Smith.

'My father always gave partners a watch such as this at the beginning of a new relationship,' said Peter Jovanovich. He meant that he felt General Cinema was the right buyer for the company. It was a risky move but allowed the two teams to cease any posturing and get down to the business of discussing how the deal could best be done.

The tenants and the landlord were only able to generate some creative options because all the interests were aired. They then came up with the innovative solution that suited both parties. If you don't declare the interests, it is difficult to get them satisfied. When the tenants took that risk, they were tapping into the concept of reciprocity that we mentioned earlier in the chapter. As human beings we tend to be more inclined to give things to those who give to us. In this case and in that of Peter Jovanovich, the act of giving something away opened the doors for the other party to be more open too. In negotiations, the giving of concessions on one side often prompts the giving of concessions from the other. There are limits to this of course: if you are negotiating with a hard positional bargainer, be careful that they are not eliciting large concessions while only making small concessions themselves.

Another pitfall is to assume that the other party is worried about the same things as us. This can lead us to think that if our fears are similar then our interests are going to clash. This is not always the case and those differing needs are often where the solution lies. It sounds simple, but find out what the other side is worried about and you may find the solution that you have both been looking for. As in the example above, this is not always easy to do if each party thinks that the stakes are high. The best negotiators are those who consistently avoid the impulse to make assumptions about the other party and are relentless in trying to find out what their underlying interests are.

3

Communication

Being a good negotiator is about being a good communicator. We know from sales research that people are more likely to buy from you if they trust you. In negotiations people are more likely to make agreements with you if they feel understood. Good communication is measured by how your message is received by the other party rather than by what you think you have delivered. You will know how it has been delivered by the response you get. You will only be able to communicate well if you enter the world of the person you are communicating with and this is why understanding values and beliefs is so important. Gathering this information will give you access to the things that are of value to the other side and allow you to communicate in a way that is most meaningful and understandable to them.

However, this is not about contrivance by telling the other side what they want to hear or using some of the tactics described here to trick them into doing something they would not otherwise do. Principled negotiation is more about attitude than it is about technique. You will get the best results if you behave naturally, but use some of the methodology we describe in this section to articulate yourself a little more clearly.

We've already talked about the fact that each party will come to the negotiating table with a different 'map of the world'. Gaining an understanding of this, then communicating that you understand will take you to the next stage which is about finding joint solutions to the problem. Flexibility is the key here; if you cannot connect with the other person, and cannot access their world at all, then you are virtually guaranteed not to make an agreement.

As a negotiator, you must take full responsibility for this communication process. Whether the other party is skilled at communication or not, you must see this as part of your job in guiding the process through to agreement and implementation. Actively and skilfully creating this connection with the person you are negotiating with is called getting 'in rapport' and is a crucial cornerstone in negotiating with integrity.

Build rapport

Building rapport is the ultimate tool for influencing and getting results from other people. Who do you get along with best? It tends to be the people who are most like you and who you like. Forget the adage that opposites attract: when it comes to powerful and effective communication in relationships, you get on best with the people you relate to most and have a deep level of understanding with.

Getting into rapport with the other person is the quickest way of creating this connection. You are in rapport with another person when there is a physical and emotional connection with the person you are communicating with; you are effectively in a state where maximum understanding occurs.

Everyone has experienced this when they are with somebody close and the communication seems to flow effortlessly. The understanding occurs on many different levels, significantly beyond the words that are spoken. Often the body language is mirrored, breathing patterns are synchronised and the pace and tone of the voice is very similar. This state can be actively induced and significantly improves the flow of information between the people involved. This is a subtle process that makes use of similar verbal phrases, pace of speaking, tonality of voice, body language and breathing. If done skilfully, it is possible to get a sense of what the other person is actually feeling.

This form of communication is based largely upon the work of the famous clinical hypnotherapist Milton Erickson. He developed the system to find the most effective ways of leading his clients into a state where they were most receptive and resourceful. He was highly successful at this and achieved some incredible results, not least in his own life where he managed his own recovery from two bouts of debilitating polio. His experiences helped him to realise the power of the unconscious mind and how it can be actively utilised to make significant changes on conscious thinking processes and in the body. Obviously we have a completely different intent here, but the set-up is the same in that it requires a level of connection and understanding between the two parties for the most effective results to be achieved.

Much of what we have talked about up to now has been about gaining an understanding of the world that the other party lives in; understanding their values, beliefs and therefore perceptions. Getting into a state of rapport is the most effective way of putting yourself in the other person's shoes as well as influencing them in a constructive way. Once you have achieved a level of rapport, you can pace and then lead the process towards finding solutions in the most efficient way possible. But this is not about manipulating the other party. Rapport is a natural state where the interchange of information is almost effortless and is at its most efficient. The power of creating rapport is that once you make a real connection with the other person you can then move to the next stages of the negotiation which are about generating options and making agreements.

Representational systems

We all experience the world through our five senses which help us to organise, store and attach meaning to our external world. Our senses can be called representational systems because reality (or the external world) and what we think is reality are not the same thing at all. There is a necessary filtering process that takes place which stops us from being over-whelmed by a constant bombardment of information. This filtering, or modelling process, includes things such as distortion, deletion and generalisation and makes it possible for us to maintain coherent models of our experiences. Understanding this means that our perceptions can be said to be accurate, based upon our own internal representational systems from which they have been derived, but are incomplete. This explains where our limitations occur and also why we have different perceptions compared to other people. Although we have five senses, there tend to be three dominant ones for most people in terms of their communication; they are visual, auditory and kines-thetic; or seeing, hearing and feeling. Everybody uses all of these systems, but most people tend to have a stronger preference for one or the other. This is useful information for us as negotiators because if we are able to identify the other person's most active sense, then we can deliberately use that to improve our communi-cation. The biggest clues to someone's preferred representational system are in the vocabulary they use.

Have a look at the boxes below and work out which system you have a preference for. It is useful to be aware of your own preferences in order to understand others', and to communicate most effectively with them.

Visual

- I can **see** how that might work.
- I've got a **mental picture** of that.
- I think our company would take a **dim view**.
- It's a pretty **short-sighted** decision.
- If only we could see **eye to eye**.
- That's pretty **clear cut**.
- I've a **hazy idea** of what you are describing.
- It **looks like** we are making progress.

Auditory

- That will get alarm bells **ringing**.
- I think we are very **tuned in**.
- My boss wanted her to **voice her** opinion.
- I want to take a minute and **bend your ear**.
- I'm hearing that **loud and clear**.
- The other side seem to be **well informed**.
- I want that **described in detail**.
- Give them time to **express themselves**.

Kinesthetic

- I want to **get to grips with** this problem.
- What this **boils down** to.
- That will take a **load off**.
- We really need to get **in touch** with them.
- Who's **pulling his strings**?

- This is something I want to **get a handle on**.
- She's a really **smooth operator**.
- I want you to **lay your cards on the table**.

Listening actively to the language is a good starting point, but the most powerful communicators use all of their senses when making a connection with others. One of the best communicators I ever met was somebody who spoke very little, but who had a profound impact on those around him. He achieved this through a powerful sense of presence — or charisma — that came from engaging people at many different levels. He created a sense of connection with people through his eye contact, body language and breathing as well as the timbre, tone and pace of his voice. When he did speak, people listened very carefully.

Leaders who make the biggest impact use this multi-faceted approach well. Even though we may not be consciously aware of what they do, we can feel moved and inspired by their communication. George Bernard Shaw said, 'In the right key one can say anything. In the wrong key, nothing: the only delicate part is the establishment of the key.' This is what understanding people's representational systems is all about. Finding the key that unlocks powerful communication for them.

If our communication is primarily with the people across the table from us, and some of these skills are only possible to utilise fully when you are negotiating face to face, identifying their dominant representational system will increase your chances of giving off the right signals so that you maximise understanding. If the others are primarily visually driven, then present things in a visually stimulating way. Get them to visualise how the solution may be, paint a picture with the words you use. If they are kinesthetic, talk about emotions, get them to imagine how it will feel if you were to make an agreement. If they are more receptive to auditory signals, listen carefully to their pace and tone, mirror this and use phraseology that will allow them to really 'hear' what you have to say. Of course all of this will require you to actively listen and observe at a level that many people do not take the time to master.

Understand body language

Interpreting other people's body language and being aware of your own is a key aspect of communication. There are a number of different studies on communication which demonstrate that when both people are totally congruent at the time of communicating, 55% of their communication will be by body language, approximately 38% will be conveyed by tonality of voice and only about 7% through the words they use. So as a means of sending signals and interpreting information, body language is a key skill to learn. Body language doesn't tell us everything and the most important aspect in gaining trust and understanding is to ensure that your communication is totally congruent.

Congruence means that your body language, words and tonality of voice are all aligned. For example, if you say 'yes' and your head is moving from side to side, there will be incongruence in your communication. I'm sure most people have experienced hearing a message and coming away from the conversation with a meaning that is completely different. Being congruent in your communication will help to build trust and generate understanding, therefore in negotiation it is important to manage your own communication style, particularly body language, and be actively aware of the people you are dealing with. Body language is the key tool in getting into rapport with others.

The most fundamental rapport-building pattern is called matching. This is where you adjust the aspects of your own body language to approximate those of the other person's behaviour. For example the position of your legs, or arms, or the tilt and angle of your head may mirror those of the person opposite you. There is a correlation between our psychology and our physiology; in other words, between our internal thinking and emotional world and the externally observable way we use our bodies.

It is useful to observe body language in other people as it will give you some idea of the things they are thinking. There are some basic patterns that are easy to spot:

- open/closed
- forward/back

Closed body language is generally characterised by crossed legs, folded arms or the body turned away and often indicates that a message is being rejected.

Open body language is generally characterised by open hands, the body facing squarely ahead and feet planted firmly on the ground pointing forwards. It usually means that a message is being received.

Forward or back tends to indicate a passive or active mode in which your communication is being received. Leaning **forward** tends to be an active stance, but means that your message may be actively received or rejected. Leaning **back** tends to indicate a passive stance where your messages may be passively absorbed or are being ignored.

Analysing these patterns of body language allows you to assess which one of four basic modes the other person is in:

- Responsive
- Receptive
- Non-responsive
- Resistant

Once you have identified the mode, you can apply some of the communication skills described in this chapter.

Open

Responsive:

- Very interested and actively receptive.
- Listening and learning about your interests, values and requirements.
- Make the agreement here, or close the sale.
- Most willing to make concessions.

Receptive:

- Interested, but not yet actively accepting.
- Time to present further information and perhaps introduce incentives.
- Give time for thinking and remaining silent.
- Ask for emotional feedback.
- Don't push, which may bring on a non-responsive mode.

Forward ——————————————— Back

Resistant:

- Actively resistant mode.
- Need to manage the emotions, diffuse any anger, provide emotional commentary.
- Ask non-directive followed by empowering questions to gather information.
- Attempt to create rapport and then pace towards receptive mode.

Non-responsive:

- Total disengagement, possibly doodling or looking out of the window.
- Do something unexpected to break the pattern; have an energy break or ask a direct question: 'I feel I've lost you, tell me what you are thinking.'
- Pace and guide into receptive mode.

Closed

Responsive

Engaged mode:
- leaning forward
- open body
- open arms
- open hands

Eager mode (sprint position):
- open legs
- feet under chair
- up on toes
- leaning forward towards speaker

On the point of agreement:
- closing papers
- putting pen down
- hands flat on table

Receptive

Listening mode:
- head tilting one way
- lots of eye contact
- nodding head
- high blink rate

Evaluating mode:
- glasses/pencil in mouth
- rubbing chin
- looking up and right
- legs crossed with ankle on knee

Attentive mode:
- may be standing
- arms behind back
- smiling
- feet apart

Non-Responsive

Disengaged mode:
- staring into space or out of window
- slumped posture
- doodling
- foot tapping

Escape mode:
- feet towards door
- looking around
- buttoning jacket

Rejection mode:
- sitting/moving back
- arms folded
- legs crossed with thigh on knee
- head down
- frowning

Defensive mode:
- may be standing, feet turned in
- hands clenched

Resistant

Wanting to speak mode:
- finger tapping
- foot tapping
- staring

Attacking mode:
- leaning forwards
- finger pointing
- fists clenched

Defiant mode:
- may be standing, hands on hips
- frowning

Lying mode:
- touching face
- hand over mouth
- pulling ear
- eyes down
- glancing at you
- shifting in seat
- looking down and to left

Matching exercises

1. Get a partner; a friend or colleague to think of a powerful emotional experience. They should not disclose to you what the experience is. For this to work they really need to mentally and emotionally re-enact the experience. Once they are there, their body will automatically adjust to reflect the state they are in. You then adjust your own body language, including stance, breathing pattern, eye-line, tilt of head, shoulders, etc. to match theirs as closely as you can. Once your body is in that position, check in with your thoughts and emotions and share those with your partner. Then make an educated guess at what you think the experience was all about. You may be surprised at how accurate you are!

2. Practise building rapport with other people, this time without any prior agreement. It could be with people at work during meetings, or it could be with people you have never met before. Notice the effect it has on the quality of your communication with them. Once you feel you have a greater connection through the matching, try to pace them and guide the communication in particular directions. Again, you may be surprised at how powerful the results are. Remember to conduct this exercise with subtlety and respect for the other person; it is not a form of manipulation.

Once you have identified the mode that the other person is in, you can then start to match by using whole or part body language, phrases or vocal qualities such as tonality, tempo, volume, timbre, or intonation. Also, things such as gestures, facial expressions, eye blinks or breathing patterns can be used that will bring you closer to making connection with them. The ongoing process of matching is called pacing; this will really build the rapport with them and the under-standing between you will significantly improve. Remember, you are not trying to reach agreement at this stage, simply to improve the communication. As we said earlier, improving the understanding does not mean that you agree with their position. Once you are pacing the other person, it is then possible to lead them by subtly changing your own body language to one of the modes that is much more open and receptive.

Set the tone of the negotiation

In my experience most people enter negotiations with a strategy of responding to what the other party says or does. There is some research in the United States which indicates that most lawyers will wait for the other side to make a proposal before they respond. There is a great opportunity in this, as if you enter the negotiation and immediately set the tone of the proceedings, then the other party is most likely to follow your lead. If you take an aggressive positional stance, you are likely to get the same in return. If you enter with the intention of establishing good communication, identifying interests and co-operating as joint problem-solvers, the other side is much more likely to take this approach also.

Often the starting point for the best relationships is to focus on the things you have in common. Conversely, when people focus on the differences or the things that are going wrong, relationships often break down. One of the key concepts of being a good negotiator is to actively manage the focus of the discussions and guide them towards the areas of benefit. This means highlighting common ground and areas of similarity, rather than the differences. It also means being solution-focused rather than problem-focused.

It is generally true that we are conditioned to look for areas of conflict and focus on what we don't want rather than what we do. If you watch the evening news for example, you will notice that all the things which are going wrong are highlighted, bringing into our consciousness the things that we don't want to happen. If you read the daily newspapers, you will find that they stand against a great number of things, and stand for very few. It is very easy to identify these things and much more challenging to find answers or solutions. However, this is your job as a negotiator. I'm not suggesting that you ignore the things that are a problem, just that you shift your focus to finding ways of reaching solutions. Don't say why things are not working, but make suggestions as to how they may work.

Human beings tend to look for and fall into patterns of behaviour, so if you open your negotiations by making generic positive statements that are difficult to disagree with, you set the tone and make unconscious suggestions that lead toward agreement. Statements such as 'We're all here to get the best possible outcome', 'There is some common ground between us' or 'We would all like to reach an amicable agreement' start to cut a groove for the thinking in the direction of agreement. This can often be observed when you see representatives reporting the progress of negotiations on the news. They will often open the interview by saying something like 'Our intention is to reach a mutually acceptable agreement as soon as possible' or 'We want to cause as little disruption as possible.' These statements are intended to elicit the support of the viewers and get them thinking that this party is doing all it can to reach agreement.

Here are some additional skills that will improve the flow of communication during the negotiation itself:

- Putting the problem before your response
- Testing understanding
- Summarising
- Labelling behaviour
- Making counter-proposals
- Diluting arguments
- Dealing with emotions
- Emotional commentary
- Dealing with emotional attacks

Put the problem before your response

When making disagreement statements, most people will tend to give the response in the order that the thoughts go through their mind. In other words, they will hear a statement from the other party that gives them a problem and they will state that they disagree with it and then proceed to give the reasons why they disagree. For example, 'That's just not going to be acceptable to us because it clashes with our busiest time of the year and we just don't have the staff available.' Making the statement in this order means that the other party will only hear the disagreement and not necessarily register the reasons. Or you may be asserting a suggestion such as 'I am thinking of putting up the rent because ...' You can be sure that whoever is receiving this message is not listening to your litany of reasons, they will be quickly calculating their own reasons for why the rent should stay the same or even be reduced.

It is much more effective if you provide your reasons first and the statement of disagreement or assertion last. For example, as the landlord looking to increase the rent, if you talk about the rise in mortgage payments, service charges and insurance first, you significantly increase the chances of the other party listening carefully as they try and follow your reasoning. The chances are that they will reach the same conclusion as you based upon your reasons, whether they like the message that is delivered or not.

No buts...

A related subtlety is to do with the use of the word 'but'. Using this word tends to negate everything that has gone before it. For example, if you say 'Yes, but ...' what you are actually saying is no, or that the conditions that follow the 'but' render the 'yes' worthless. In effect the recipient will be listening to your conditions and not the 'yes'. Better to make your approach by saying 'Yes.' (full stop, new paragraph)

'... And the other information I would like you to consider is ...' This is a much more effective and inclusive way of structuring your response. The 'yes' will be heard as well as the other factors that form the conditions. Remember that we are dealing with perceptions here and your 'yes' is very often in response to the way that the other party sees things. In our example of the landlord and tenant discussion, the tenant's response could be 'Yes, I can see why you feel the need to increase the rent and the other things that should also be considered are ...' and the tenant may go on to explain that they have always looked after the place, that similar properties in the area are asking less, that they are willing to stay longer if the rent is kept low.

Testing understanding

Regularly testing that your understanding of what they have said allows you to clarify, summarise, get further responses from the other party and also slow down the process if necessary.

'Let me just check if I understand you correctly ...'

By reflecting your understanding of the things they have said, you will ensure there is less ambiguity and also get the other party to make agreement statements. The more agreement statements people make, the more you will feel like you are making progress. This also uses the social reinforcement trigger we talked about earlier as you are getting people to make a public commitment to your summary. Of course, testing understanding is key if you think there is genuine misunderstanding and this is better dealt with as it arises. This links in with good implementation planning, which will be discussed a little later.

Testing understanding can also be used to effectively challenge people's perceptions. Often people will say things like *'Your people are always late with your orders.'* You should challenge how specific they are being:

'Are you saying everyone is late all of the time?'

'Well, no, not everyone, it's usually the electrical department.'

'Is that all people in the electrical department?'

'I suppose not, we tend to deal with Joe, and he is often late, but Fred and Harry are generally okay.'

'And does that tend to be all of the time, or is it at particular times?'

'The problem is generally during overhauls. I know Joe is the busiest, but it's still causing us some problems.'

'So let me just make sure I understand where the problem is; it is the speed of Joe's response in the electrical department during overhauls that is giving you most cause for concern.'

'Yes.'

'Well that's very helpful and allows me to do something about it straight away. If I came back to you with a proposal by this time next week, would that help to solve your problems?'

'Yes, definitely.'

When people are frustrated, they tend to generalise about things and make negative associations with all sorts of unrelated matters. It is important to manage that perception by being as specific as possible and removing any ambiguity or confusion.

Summarising
Summarising is closely related to testing understanding, but also allows you to create some stage-gates during the negotiation process. Very simply it is

a pause in the proceedings where the things that have already been agreed are repeated to ensure that everybody's understanding is consistent. The brain likes chunks of information that are related to or associated with things that have already been assimilated. By regularly summarising you are 'banking' the things that have already been agreed, clarifying the nature of the agreements and making sure that everyone's perceptions are on track. Research on learning and brain functioning indicates that recall and understanding are at their greatest between 20 and 50 minutes after an event. If possible make the summaries coincide with any natural comfort or energy breaks you take. Plan the summaries in and complete them at the end and the beginning of the break periods. So if you have a negotiation that lasts for a couple of hours, plan at least one break which will allow you to summarise the things already agreed. You may simply say 'Just before we move on to other things, let's just make sure we are clear on the things already agreed ...' then go on to list the key elements of the agreements and elicit everybody's acknowledgement. This is not an opportunity to renegotiate the things already talked about, so it needs to be carefully managed and presented, but will help everybody feel that progress is being made.

Labelling your behaviour

Behaviour-labelling is a communication skill that signposts the move you are about to make and allows the other party to prepare and maximise receptivity. It is a little like the evening news concept where they tell you what they are going to tell you, tell you, and then finish by telling you what they have told you! In negotiations this provides an advance signal for the verbal content you are about to deliver. For example:

> 'Can I just ask a couple of questions at this point to make sure I understand what you mean?'

or

> 'Do you mind if I express some thoughts about what you've just described?'

This is good interactive communication as you are preparing the other party for receiving information rather than delivering. Wording the statements as questions will generally elicit 'permission' to interrupt from the person you are addressing; they will switch to listening mode and are more likely to hear what you say.

Making counter-proposals

Some research on negotiation indicates that making immediate counter-proposals to the other party's proposal is more likely to be seen as a blocking or disagreement statement rather than being heard as a proposal at all. A more effective way of approaching the presentation of your own arguments is by acknowledging the validity of the other side's argument first. You may say something like 'I think your arguments are actually very valid, let me see if I understand exactly what you are proposing ...' If you are able to demonstrate that you understand where they are coming from, you are much more likely to have your counter-arguments listened to. In fact, if you are able to present their case more articulately than they can and highlight the strengths, before challenging it with your own arguments, there is a strong likelihood that your arguments will be accepted.

In a real case where residents were concerned about safety while construction of a new railway station was underway, they were helped to reach a satisfactory agreement by taking the following approach:

The representative for the residents opened by saying, *'I can see where the construction manager is coming from actually. I understand his point that they have few options for the route for the construction vehicles and the only other access point would be through Theakston Green, which would create even more disruption than coming through Beckley Circle. I also take his point that once construction is completed we will all benefit from the improved rail access. I understand his arguments and I think they are valid. However, we also have a very strong case and I would like to outline our concerns ...'*

By demonstrating a good understanding of the other side's case you will add more weight to your own proposals as well as stand a much better chance of having them heard by the other party. This may be even more important if you are presenting your case to a third party, as in this case, where the matter was being arbitrated by the local councillor.

Whoever the other side is, they are entitled to have their opinion heard, whether you agree with the message or not. In hearing and demonstrating your understanding of the message, you will create a measure of satisfaction in the other party and you will open the lines of communication much more effectively. It will also help to avoid things such as defend/attack spirals or tit-for-tat behaviour which does not lead you towards efficient agreement-making. If one side feels as though their interests are being ignored, deliberately misunderstood or negated then they will tend to feel the need to defend their position or attack the other side. What one person perceives as a legitimate defence, the other side may see as an unwarranted attack. The responses will then be made with increasing intensity and the spiral continues. Making a conscious effort to understand and validate the other side's interests is a communication skill that does not cost you anything to adopt and can provide the foundation for making an elegant agreement.

Diluting arguments

Additionally, many negotiators believe that it is an advantage to provide as many reasons as possible for strengthening their argument. This can actually dilute the case. You will have much more impact if your arguments are focused on a small number of key issues. In the example above, the spokesperson for the residents actually concentrated on the safety of the children in Beckley Circle and cited a couple of very specific examples of near-misses.

'Sally Jones of number 15 was nearly run over by one of your trucks travelling at over 40 mph on the 12 September at 16.00, just as she was returning home from school. The following Wednesday Timmy Smith was also saved from serious injury; his mother pulled him out of the path of one of your dumper trucks that mounted the kerb at 8.50 in the morning.'

There were plenty of other less serious complaints by many of the local residents that could have been listed exhaustively, but the argument was made strongest by focusing on those things that would be understood and also appeal to the other side's interests. This is also an opportunity to influence the other party's perceptions. In this case the site manager cited scheduling pressures for the speed and frequency of the traffic through this residential street.

The residents' spokesperson countered by saying, *'I've already explained that we fully understand the commercial pressures you are under and the benefits we will all get from the completed project, but surely you are not saying that those things are more important than the safety of our children?'*

Clearly the site manager had to concede this point and his perception was broadened beyond that of the time and money pressures that he was focused on before.

We talked earlier about repetition helping the assimilation of information through the use of summaries and testing understanding. Interestingly, there is some evidence that repeating an argument can increase the degree to which it is retained, but the limits of this are well defined. In 1978, The Huthwaite Research group, led by Neil Rackham and John Carlisle examined the behaviour of professional negotiators, including union and management representatives and contract managers. The information was gathered during real negotiations, including planning sessions, for groups that were classified as either 'skilled' because they had been identified as such by peers, or 'average' because they failed to meet the skilled criteria or because no data was available on them. This research demonstrated that, beyond two repetitions, saturation occurs which can lead to a rejection and possibly dislike of the message. When presenting your arguments, less is more; choose your strongest points and repeat only a couple of times until the message has been heard and understood.

Dealing with emotions

Because you are dealing with human beings, often the emotions are more important than the words used. Even people who know each other well often have difficulty communicating accurately and effectively. It is therefore even more of a challenge for people who are strangers to express themselves without misunderstanding. Consider that miscommunication may be a result of genuinely not knowing how to express something or it may be a deliberate attempt to mislead. Negotiators don't always mean what they say, or say what they mean. This process becomes even more difficult when you introduce the concept of dealing with emotions. Emotions can help or hinder the process of communication in all relationships, so they must be dealt with.

To manage anything with skill requires awareness and you need to be aware of your own emotions before you can apply any tactics for managing the emotions of other people. You need to be in touch enough, in the moment, to judge exactly how you are feeling. Notice if you are becoming anxious, angry, nervous or excited. If they are getting in the way, make your emotions explicit.

Emotional commentary

Skilled negotiators are often thought of as people who keep their feelings to themselves, who play their cards close to their chests. However, making emotions explicit can often clear the air, provide breakthroughs in the event of deadlock or demonstrate how seriously you are taking any particular matter. This is not to say that you should indulge in those feelings in a way that is negative or damaging, but good negotiators tend to provide information about their emotions in the form of some kind of feelings commentary. For example:

> *'I'm beginning to feel a little uncomfortable about some of the suggestions you are making, I wonder if you could help me make sure I've heard you correctly.'*

> *'I'm feeling somewhat confused at the moment, could you please help to clarify a few things for me ...'*

Often just expressing the emotions is enough to clear a blockage and gives the other side information about how you're feeling about the negotiation's progress.

Dealing with emotional attacks

Occasionally, the other side will react by attacking you emotionally. It is important that you stay in control of situations like this and try to direct this energy as constructively as possible. Do not respond to emotional outbursts with an outburst of your own, but stay focused on what you are trying to achieve. Your response can be summarised by following the five R's:

1. **Receive** without comment or emotional reaction. Allow the other party to let off steam and initially do not respond.

2. **Relate** to their feelings and show genuine concern. Often making a gesture that sounds like an apology can diffuse the energy of the situation. *'I'm sorry that you feel like that, it certainly wasn't my intention.'* Again, just to be clear, this is not about agreeing with their reaction, or accepting blame, it is simply making a statement of concern showing you understand how they feel.

3. **Reflect** what they have said calmly to show you heard and allow them to hear it.

4. **Request** from them the action they are expecting from you.

5. **Review** everything you have heard and respond objectively.

Consider breaking the pattern of the negotiation at this point. Make some kind of gesture such as buying them a coffee or at least taking a break. This is not ignoring the issue, it just allows some time for reflection and a change of environment which may bring some fresh insight. When you regroup, deal with the issue, then once the energy has been diffused you can perhaps discuss it a little more objectively.

In situations where you are dealing with emotions, always talk about yourself and not the other party. Frame your statements in terms of how you are affected and how you feel. This does not allow any opportunity for further disagreement statements about your response as no-one can dispute the things that you are feeling. For example, instead of saying *'You don't understand me.'* You could say *'I don't feel understood.'*

Communication: summary box

- Separate the people issues from the substance of the negotiation.
- Know your own style.
- Use all forms of communication including body language and verbal skills to build a bridge of understanding and create rapport.
- Be creative, not reactive: take the initiative and set the tone for the negotiation.
- Actively and constructively deal with the emotions; yours and the other party's.

Case study

The drunk had been in the baker's shop for two hours, shouting at staff and customers and generally causing a nuisance when Jason, the local street warden arrived. Repeated attempts to remove the drunk had all failed and the situation was in danger of getting even worse.

The London street wardens do a difficult job. They are there to integrate into the community and provide a reassuring presence in the neighbourhood, but this often involves dealing with some of the most challenging members of the community, such as those living on the street and the odd drunk. The incidents they have to deal with can be distressing for the general public and disruptive for local businesses, but are often too low priority for the police. Unlike the police force, the street warden has no official powers to arrest or detain and therefore all situations have to be managed using diplomacy and persuasion. My friend Jason is very good at his job and is often asked to mediate where other people have failed.

In the baker's shop, the drunk, who was now becoming increasingly distressed, had been confronted by both the manager of the shop and another warden. He was refusing to budge and was standing in the corner in a highly agitated state when Jason arrived.

Knowing that the man had been confronted by everyone else, Jason took a different approach. He approached with very passive body language; he opened his arms in front of him in a wide, friendly gesture and said, 'Hello mate, do you mind if I sit down here?' The drunk was momentarily surprised that this person wasn't attempting to attack him, so he gave his consent. Jason sat down at a table and leant backwards. In a quiet voice he said, 'You look really upset; tell me what has been happening.'

Of course the man continued his tirade at first until Jason said, 'You know, you're hurting my ears with all this shouting; sit here and explain properly to me what the problem is.' Somewhat taken aback that somebody was asking him questions rather than shouting at him, the man sat down at the table. He explained that he had come in for a cup of tea and had spilled his drink over another customer. Jason continued to ask detailed questions, repeating the answers to confirm them.

'So you came in for a quiet drink and ended up spilling it over somebody. I know it happens. But did you apologise to the poor lady you spilled the drink on?'

'Yes, I said I was sorry, but he still wasn't happy with me ...' he pointed to the shop manager.

'So, let me get this right. You spilled the drink, but then apologised and they still had a go at you?' repeated Jason. He continued, 'To be honest, that kind of thing has happened to me, so I can understand why you are upset, particularly if you have apologised.'

The drunk launched into another string of abuse directed at the manager, but Jason put his hands out again and said, 'You've told him how upset you are already, what is it you want from him?'

'I want to fight him!' stated the drunkard.

'Look,' said Jason. 'You know he's just doing his job don't you? He's probably got a wife and kids at home and he's trying to provide a good service for his customers. You've told him how upset you are and I'm sure he understands.'

The drunk conceded this was probably true and now seemed a little unsure of what to do.

'Come on, let's go ...' Jason suggested. The man got up unsteadily and they started to walk out of the shop. When Jason told me this he said that he walked a little like the drunk as they left the shop!

The drunk did swear at the manager again on the way out, but then Jason broke his pattern once more by suggesting, 'You know, if I were you I'd go to the park on such a lovely day. Where are your friends?'

The man thought for a second and then said, 'You know, I think I'll just go home ...'

Analysis

Jason's intervention took about five minutes from entering the shop to leaving with the drunken man. Compare this with the previous two hours, during which the incident had gradually escalated into an angry situation where all parties were locked in a stalemate.

The first thing that Jason did was to approach the issue with a particular frame of mind, separating the people from the problem. Of course the man's condition and attitude was a significant factor in the situation and a big part of the problem, but the previous attempts had been a confrontational battle of wills where one person would need to lose for the other to win.

In most cases if you approach any negotiation with an aggressive confrontational position, you are most likely to get exactly the same in return. Jason did not entangle his own ego with the problem and was therefore able to focus on what would provide the best and most efficient solution. He didn't take the situation personally and looked at it from the point of view of a problem to solve. Often as human beings we have a need to be right, so if the negotiation becomes a battle to prove yourself right and the other person wrong, both parties risk losing.

The approach of the first warden and the manager was to point out to the drunk that his behaviour was unacceptable and that he must concede by leaving the shop. Most of us would probably agree with this, but remember that people do things for reasons and the drunk felt he had a perfect right to demand an apology from the shop manager. The man's judgement was clearly impaired by alcohol, but actually, when we become emotional in the heat of a negotiation, our perception is rarely perfectly balanced.

The first practical thing that Jason needed to do for any communication to take place, was to make a connection with the man. He did this by showing that he wasn't a threat, through his facial expressions, tone of voice and body language. He also demonstrated that he was willing to understand things from the man's point of view. Rather than taking the moral high ground and telling him what to do, he asked lots of questions and demonstrated understanding.

It is important to remember that understanding is not the same as agreeing. Jason's focus was on getting a solution, not making a moral judgement. Simply getting into the other person's world can give an insight into how they are thinking and what is likely to move them in a different direction. Once some communication, a level of trust and some understanding had been established, Jason was able to alter the man's perception by giving him an insight as to where the other party was coming from. When he explained that the manager was just doing his job, the drunk could see beyond his own perception of the situation and he conceded that his was not the only point of view.

This concept of separating the people issues from the problem at hand is a key concept in any negotiation, otherwise the ego and will of the individuals becomes hopelessly entangled with the real issues. Once he had established a level of rapport with the drunk, Jason was able to lead him from the shop without any resistance.

Another important thing that Jason did was to deliberately break the flow of the man's thinking by doing or saying something unexpected. His approach threw the man off guard because the current environment was one of attack and defend. Jason did neither of these things and created a space for another approach to take place. This is called a pattern interrupt; it momentarily confuses the brain so that it has to pause and look for further information about what will happen next. It can be a useful technique to use in negotiations as deadlocks can often be broken by taking a different direction. Actively look for opportunities to change the other party's perception of you by doing something that they do not expect.

Many of these things happen in quick succession at a very subtle level and often without the other party being consciously aware of it. This is the skill in powerful communication: making the communication work well even without the other person's knowledge or participation. Even though he would not have been able to explain what was happening, the drunk man was conscious of the different experience he was having when dealing with Jason's different style of communication.

4

Generating Options

*I*magine going into a restaurant and preparing to order some food. The waiter says, 'We don't have a menu, just tell me what you would like and I'll tell you if we can do it.'

You make a couple of suggestions and the waiter replies, 'Sorry, we don't do any of those, try again.'

This is the approach we often take to negotiations when we immediately search for the one single solution that will meet everybody's interests. This is particularly the approach of the positional bargainer who says, 'Make me an offer and I'll tell you if it's acceptable to me.'

In the restaurant, the first thing you suggest that the kitchen has, is what you end up with. It may not have been the thing you really felt like, but if it's the only option you've identified, you end up with it all the same. It's the same with the positional approach to making agreements. If you get drawn into that game, the first thing suggested that is acceptable to the other party may not be the best option for you. There might have been a more elegant solution if you had had other options to choose from.

Just like perusing the choices at a buffet before you choose, if you have a range of options, you stand a much better chance of finding a solution that meets your needs. This is to be solution-focused. Being problem-focused is not that effective in negotiations. It would be like telling the server behind the buffet that you're allergic to this, that makes you fat and you really don't like anything with anchovies. The server waits with the serving utensils, getting frustrated, and will eventually say, 'Well, that's all very interesting, but tell me what it is you do want ...' It is only when you shift your focus that you will get the results you are looking for.

The thinking environment created by our waiter without a menu is one of single-solution thinking. It is much more effective if you go through a process of idea generation and evaluation before having the opportunity of making an informed decision. However, when you are in the heat of a negotiation and feeling under pressure, it is seldom easy to start generating creative options. Option generation should be carried out either during your personal preparation phase or later, with the other side. In either case, it is important to separate the process of generating ideas from the process of selection and deciding. This clear demarcation between stages takes off some pressure and allows you to be as creative and unconventional as possible.

Creatively generating options is one of the most important things you can do as a negotiator and one of the areas most often overlooked. For this reason this process must be well controlled and planned in advance.

Expanding the pie

By generating options we can expand the pie before we cut it. It is easy to fall into thinking that more for you means less for me or that the only issue on the table is that of money. For example, when negotiating the purchase of a car, price is clearly one of the elements to be agreed, but the scope of options can be significantly broadened by including things such as servicing, road tax, warranty, part exchange, finance and insurance.

Rather than seeing the negotiation as a fixed pie, where the price of the car is the only consideration, and the more the dealer gets, the less the discount there is for you, you could discuss other options including the variables above, many of which may be of low cost to the seller, but high value to you, before agreeing the price. This could mean including an extended warranty, road tax, the first service or beneficial terms for any financing. Remember that you are always looking for ways to identify and satisfy the interests of the other party. It may be that the salesman's performance is measured in terms of the figures that make up the sale price of the car and that he will be much more flexible regarding the other variables. Be constantly looking for opportunities to expand the scope of the agreement and you will significantly increase the chances of finding creative, elegant and perhaps innovative solutions in your negotiations.

The process of generating options
There are a couple of places that option generation should be undertaken; the first is in your own planning and the second is during the negotiation. If you've done the first well, then the second will be much easier. Rackham and Carlisle's research into the behaviour of skilled negotiators, mentioned earlier, found that both the skilled and the average group spent about the same amount of time on planning, but that there were marked differences on how the time was spent. The successful group were found to have spent twice the amount of time as the average group exploring a wide range of their own options as well as a wide spectrum of options which the other party might introduce.

This process of creating options gives you more variety on the buffet table when it comes to making your selection, but it is clearly important to include those items that the other party will want to choose too. It is all too easy to make premature judgements about things because people think that they already have the answer. If you already think you know what to do, you will go into any communication with a closed mind. The problem is, if the other party comes to the table with the same attitude, but with a different solution in mind, then deadlock may be the result. Skilled negotiators tend to spend much more time gathering information and staying convergent as long as possible before they diverge upon potential solutions.

In fact, in the same research, Rackham and Carlisle found that the skilled group of negotiators spent time seeking more than twice as much information as the average group. Also, while both groups explored possible areas of conflict, the skilled group paid more than three times as much attention to finding areas of common ground with the other party. This goes back to the importance of identifying the values and interests of the party you are negotiating with. Without putting yourself in their shoes, it is impossible to generate options that may satisfy those interests. When you invent options, think in terms of making it as easy as possible for them to say yes. If in your planning sessions you have managed to identify their interests and your options satisfy these, and you have anticipated their objections, it becomes very difficult for them to say no.

Brainstorming

By definition, inventing options means that you will have to come up with things that are not already in your head. Brainstorming is a great way to do this. It is obviously a creative process and as such should not be constrained by too many rules; however, here are some suggestions that may make the session as productive as possible:

1. **Get the environment right**. The brainstorming needs to be separated from the other parts of the negotiation process. This means that it is often helpful for it to take place in a different location than your normal offices or meeting rooms. This may help to create a more relaxed atmosphere, particularly if it is in a hotel, people perhaps dress down or it is done over informal drinks. Sit people on one side of the table facing the problem, not each other. This should be seen as a metaphor where the team are united against a problem rather than behaving as adversaries across the table. Appoint a facilitator; this will ensure that the ground rules are followed and that everyone makes a contribution. Make sure that the right people are there. This should include those who understand the problem, but also individuals who are on the outside of the negotiation process and are perhaps able to see things a little more objectively.

2. **Agree the purpose of the session**. Once you have the right environment and the right team, it will be necessary to agree a purpose statement. Be clear that brainstorming is about generating options, not about finding the definitive solution. If people feel that any suggestion made will be seized as an admission or acceptance of that suggestion, then

they are less likely to take risks or be creative in their thinking. This is particularly the case if you do any brainstorming with the other side. Often the most radical thinking produces new solutions, so this kind of environment must be actively created by agreeing what you are trying to achieve and by the facilitator keeping the discussion within those guidelines. Your purpose statement should be sharp enough to reflect what you would like in your hand when you leave the room.

3. **Brainstorm**. Be creative. Attack the problem from every angle and play with a few ideas that in other circumstances would not have been considered. The facilitator should ensure that everyone makes some kind of contribution and that all ideas are treated fairly. It is important that no criticism takes place at this point and it's the facilitator's job to ensure that this is strictly enforced. If people feel ideas will be judged at this stage, then it will stifle contributions. All ideas should be recorded, preferably on a flip chart where everyone can see what is being written. The facilitator should clarify the contribution if necessary but then write down the idea in the contributor's words. It is probably a good idea not to attribute ideas to individuals at this stage so that the finished list is owned by the team as a whole. Earlier we talked about the power of questions and how asking the right questions can completely shift our focus or change our perspective. Brainstorming is a good time to use such techniques, particularly

the possibility questions we mentioned earlier: 'What if we included this in the agreement, how would that change things?' 'How would the other side feel if ...'

4. **Sift and select**. Signal the end of the brainstorming session. Start the process of identifying the ideas that show most promise by perhaps putting an asterisk against those that you feel are best. This is still not the deciding stage, it is about creating as many ideas as possible that are different to each other so that you maximise the negotiating space.

5. **Improve**. This list of the most promising ideas should then be strengthened. Think in terms of the interests on both sides that need to be satisfied and how practical the ideas are to implement on the ground. It may be possible to weave some of the concepts from the weaker ideas into the stronger ones to make them a little more robust or creative. The output from this stage of the process should be a list of very different, strong ideas that can then be evaluated before they are taken forward.

6. **Evaluate and decide**. Even at this stage of the process the objective should not be to narrow down to a single idea that you will take forward. Rather you should have a range of options from which solutions can be drawn during the negotiation itself. Consider using some kind of evaluation model such as the one below to provide a list of suggestions with different strengths.

The following is a simple evaluation tool that allows you to put any criteria in the columns. It provides some structure to your thinking to assess the relative strengths of the options you have generated. The scores in the boxes will need to be agreed amongst the whole group so that a consensus is reached. For each of the columns, think in the broadest terms: 'ease to do' should consider implementation and ongoing maintenance as well as any short-term issues; 'cost' should not just be money, but also the emotional, public relations or environmental cost. When completing the 'effect on interest' boxes, ensure that you put yourself in the shoes of the other party so that you get the most accurate and honest evaluation of how they would perceive the option.

These steps have been written from the point of view of brainstorming during your planning phase. If you have a relationship with the other side that you feel is open enough, you could consider brainstorming with them. This obviously carries a higher risk of disclosing confidential information or mistaking an option for an offer, but can be worth it in terms of strengthening the relationship and producing suggestions that will relate to both sets of interests. If you do brainstorm with the other side, it is very important that the session is identified as being distinct from the negotiation. In other words, step 2 above should be explicitly agreed and perhaps a specific time-scale allowed for this process so that it is seen as being separate from the negotiation where the objective is to seek agreements.

Option/idea	Ease to do	Cost	Effect on their interests	Effect on our interests	Totals	The best choice

Mark 1–4, where **1 = Low** (Easy to do, low cost, little effort) and **4 = High** (Hard to do, high costs, huge effort).
The best choices have the lowest marks.

Manage the environment

The environmental factors in negotiations are very important and skilled negotiators leave as little to chance as possible. This should include general environmental factors such as where the negotiation is held, as well as more specific factors such as lighting and chair positions. See the physical environment as being reflective of your mental and emotional attitude towards the negotiation and the other party; a metaphor for your personal approach and be aware that the physical reinforces the psychological.

Where to negotiate

When you negotiate with integrity you are not trying to intimidate the other party into doing something they otherwise would not do. This approach does not give each party the most appropriate outcome or make for lasting agreements. For this reason, try to choose a location for the negotiation that reflects this sense of openness and co-operation, that is relatively neutral and not designed to be intimidating. I spent some years conducting interviews for people looking to join the company I worked for. These young people were often the brightest in their field and we wanted to make sure we were choosing people who not only would perform well for the company, but also satisfy their own needs, so that we would build lasting relationships with them. We used a method called 'behavioural event interviewing', which looked at real examples in their lives, rather than hypothetical or imagined circumstances, so that we were exploring genuine reactions and behaviours to actual events.

We got consistently good results this way because we created an environment where the candidates could express themselves honestly and we were able to quickly identify whether there was a fit between personal needs and company values. We found that it was totally counter-productive to place people under intimidating circumstances where they were deliberately tripped up or confused. In this latter environment, we found out little about how the candidates felt or thought and the evidence bore little relation to how they performed under real working circumstances later on. If your negotiations are about building long-term relationships, then some of these environmental factors apply in the same way. If you deliberately set out to intimidate the other party so that they are manipulated into agreements, then you will find you get problems at the closing or implementation stages, or that you will have damaged a working relationship somewhere in the future. Consider holding the negotiations in a hotel, or if it needs to be in one or other of the parties' offices, in a conference room rather than a personal office. This doesn't give one party the advantage of being on home turf and in a position to control the environment for their own ends. It also means that you are less likely to be interrupted and allows you to focus on the issues at hand.

Managing remote negotiations
Although much of what we talked about under communication skills relied upon the negotiations taking

place face to face, many negotiations now do take place in other environments such as over the telephone and through video conferencing. These circumstances do present challenges of their own that will need managing even more carefully than if you are present, as the potential for misunderstanding without cues such as facial expressions and other forms of body language is much greater. It is still possible to apply some of the techniques described here, including some of the communication skills, but they are much more difficult to control. For example, getting in rapport with somebody on the telephone is possible through matching tonality and pace of voice. As mentioned earlier, the words you use convey much less than the pitch, timbre and tone of your voice. If you are negotiating over the phone, or over video, then you will need to be much more aware of how you use your voice. Add some emotion and interest for the listener by adding some light and shade; good use of your breath will help you to control volume and tonality. If you breathe deeply when speaking you are able to give yourself more power which will come across to the listener. Ensure that the emotions you are conveying through your voice are congruent with the words you are using as the other person will almost certainly detect any inconsistency, so trust and understanding will be undermined. Skills such as summarising and testing understanding are much more important when you do not have the benefit of other communication cues to build a fuller picture. Pause often, paraphrase what you think you have heard or summarise what has been agreed. Check that your understanding matches the other party's and be honest if you do not understand or are confused.

Because there is less information exchange over the phone or video the words you use are also of paramount importance. We mentioned the use of the word 'but' earlier; avoid this as much as possible and replace it with the word 'and'. This will come across as much more agreeable and solution-focused. Avoid the use of the word 'try' as it implies that you think you will not succeed and that may be interpreted as a lack of commitment by the listener. There are much more powerful words to use, such as 'will' and it will help to convey a sense of power, commitment and determination that will help to build trust, confidence and understanding with the other party. Language is a very important medium that conveys much more than simple facts and should be considered a tool to be used as skilfully as possible.

As well as your verbal skills, your listening skills will need to be much more attuned when you lack the benefit of real-time physical contact. Make sure that the other person knows you are actively listening by using encouraging noises such as 'I see', 'Mmm', 'Aha', and 'Yes'. If they cannot see you nodding, making eye contact or any of the other signals that you convey to show you are listening and understanding, then these messages will need to be delivered in other ways. Don't be too afraid of silences either, as often well-timed pauses give time for thought, evaluation and perhaps further explanation. People do tend to like to fill silences, particularly on the telephone, and by providing the space, you may get more information from the other party if they feel obliged to fill the silences. You may find that an even greater use of questions will help the flow of information under these circumstances as it will help to clarify and gather information for everybody listening.

It is crucial that a good wrap-up or summary is made towards the end of the conversation to ensure that everybody leaves with exactly the same understanding. Many of the communication skills used over the phone or during a video conference are very similar to those used in face-to-face negotiations, but they must be used much more skilfully and actively to make the less information-rich environment yield the results you want.

Control the local environment

As well as the location of the negotiation, the immediate environment should be given some consideration during your planning and preparation stage. For example, if the parties sit across the table from each other, this tends to reinforce the attitude that you are adversaries facing each other and your barrier to moving forwards is the person in front of you. However, if you both sit on the same side of the table and face the problem which may be written on a flipchart in front of you, this reinforces the attitude that you are joint problem-solvers looking for solutions together.

If this feels too informal or friendly, then sit across the corner of the table from the other party. This way, you will maintain some professional formality, but be in a much less confrontational stance.

Make the environment formal but relaxed. You want to reinforce the fact that you are there for serious business, but also want to encourage openness and creativity. Make sure there are enough resources such as flip charts and pens and make them visible and available as though you fully expect them to be used.

Manage energy and attention

In discussing building relationships above, we mentioned that negotiators are human beings before anything else. There are physical and energetic factors that can be actively managed that will have an impact on the quality of the process. Be aware that people's energy and concentration levels will fluctuate throughout the day and you can use this knowledge to manage them skilfully. Each person's energy 'peaks' occur at different times, so you need to observe if this is having an effect on the success of the negotiation. There is a piece of research in which 1500 negotiators were asked to report on their own energy levels throughout the day. The results indicated that most people are at their best energetically and creatively in the morning. This study found that 1200 of the 1500 peaked early in the day.

These results are consistent with other research in the area of child performance at school which led some European schools to reorganise timetables to start early in the day and finish earlier in the afternoon. There is also some evidence, however, that a smaller

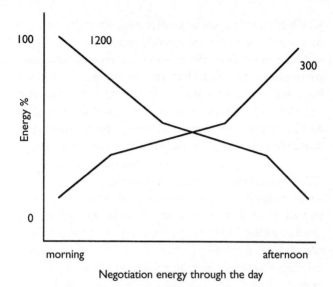

Negotiation energy through the day

number of people, 300 in the negotiation research, do perform better in the afternoon. This would perhaps suggest that you should schedule your meetings in the morning and if you are not getting much success in the first few hours of the meeting, break and then re-schedule the meeting for later in the day.

Do also recognise that there is a pattern to the profile of attention spans during the day. The levels tend to decline as time goes on, which means that you should actively plan a number of adjournments through the day. However, attention tends to fall faster in each successive session, so if you are going to plan longer sessions, make them the earlier ones.

Be flexible about the sequence

One of the other approaches observed in skilful negotiators is their ability to be flexible about when particular issues are addressed during the negotiation. In contrast, average performers tended to be more rigid in following a fixed sequence. It is a little like the difference between following a fixed path to get from A to B or being familiar enough with the terrain to pick the path that is most efficient depending upon prevailing conditions. A skilled negotiator is someone who is able to read the map and the compass effectively so that all of the key issues can be navigated flexibly along the way. This means that during your preparation you will need to be clear about where the key issues lie and what are the priorities, then be sure that they are on the agenda without being too concerned where they come in the list.

One related issue that merits a mention here is note-taking. Minutes of every meeting should be taken and agreed afterwards, but I have learnt that it is always worthwhile taking your own notes. I take notes of every conversation I have, including telephone conversations that occur before the negotiations. This is more about clarity than protection, although it is useful for both. It is an impressive relationship-building tool if you can come back at a later stage to somebody and recount some detail about your last interaction. This will send a clear message about your ability to listen, the importance of the relationship and your attention to detail.

Generating options: summary box

- Find a creative space for generating options.
- If a menu of choices doesn't exist, then create one.
- Expand the pie before you cut it.
- Consider brainstorming with the other side.
- Manage the environmental factors to give the best outcomes.

Case study

The city contract for waste disposal was up for renewal in a seaside town in California. It is usual for local authority contracts to go out to competitive tender so that the best use of public money is made. June Oliver was the negotiator for an Arizona-based disposal company and was determined to win the contract. Despite being faced with stiff competition from other haulage companies, she managed to win the contract with the city council, even though her bid was $5 per ton higher than her competitors. Oliver managed this because she understood the interests of the client and presented a unique and creative option that satisfied these interests.

In her spare time June Oliver is a keen surfer. Because of this, she knew that the beaches in the town were a significant source of tourist income as well as a factor affecting property values. She also knew that the beaches were slowly eroding away. The waste disposal sites that her company used were in the Arizona desert and were of course surrounded by an abundance of sand. When she made her bid to the city, she did not simply offer to remove the waste from town, she also suggested that when her lorries made the return trip, they did so full of pure desert sand that could be used to replenish the eroding beaches. It was this creative option that demonstrated her understanding of the client's real needs and won her the contract, despite her bid being higher than her competitors'.

Examples abound about Donald Trump's negotiation exploits. Trump, the property and gambling mogul, was planning to construct his flagship building, Trump Tower on Fifth Avenue, New York. In order to do this he needed air rights over the famous jewellery store, Tiffany and Company. Tiffany's was in a classic building and was run by a very traditional New Yorker by the name of Walter Hoving. The story goes that Trump was willing to pay $5million for the rights, but thought that Hoving would turn him down on the grounds that aesthetic integrity was to be maintained on that part of Fifth Avenue.

Trump prepared for the meeting by getting his architect to make two different models of Trump Tower. He brought them both along to the meeting to discuss the air rights. One of them was an elegant 50-storey building that he said was his favoured option. He would construct this one, which was an appropriate neighbour for Hoving's high-class jewellery store, if he was able to get the air rights. The second model was a hideous building that he insisted the authorities would force him to build if he didn't get the agreement. This 50-storey building had tiny, mesh-filled windows, all facing the Tiffany building. The two models sat side by side on Hoving's desk. 'These are your options,' said Trump. 'It's up to you to choose ...' Walter Hoving got the message and agreed to the air rights.

Analysis

Options can be used in a number of different ways. In the first example, we see a case where options can be used skilfully to generate solutions that otherwise would not exist. The officials in the city council thought that they wanted the cheapest waste disposal contract possible, but cost and value are different things. June Oliver managed to expand the pie that the city officials were looking at, even if they didn't know they were looking for those options, and provide a solution that was of low cost to her but of high value to the client. The cost of hauling sand to the city on the return journey for the waste disposal company was very low, but it was of very high value to the city officials.

The same can be said for the tenant and landlord negotiation described in Chapter 2. The cost of painting the apartment for the tenant was actually very low, but of high value to the landlord. The tenants would only have to pay for the paint and would get the benefit of a freshly painted flat. It would have cost the landlord significantly more to employ a painting contractor who would have charged much more than the option he ended up with.

Always approach negotiations looking for options that may provide low-cost, high-value solutions. Also look for opportunities for mutual gain even if they take some seeking out. This is not the easy or obvious way of approaching agreement and one of the reasons that negotiating well is a skill to be practised and learnt. We are taught to look at negotiations where the options on the table are relatively fixed and therefore if you get more, I get less. It is much harder to look beyond the obvious and seek options that will benefit both parties.

In the situation I described at the beginning of the book when you completed the questionnaire to assess your natural negotiation style, it was easiest and most obvious to think in terms of winners and losers or of how the ten thousand pounds would be split. The approach that is much less obvious is the one where you look beyond making compromises or creating winners and losers and look for the options that will satisfy interests on all sides. So, generating options can be used as a creative deal-maker or deadlock-breaker in the hands of skilled negotiators.

In the example of Donald Trump, some may feel that options were presented aggressively. This is not the most positive use of options, but more of a leverage tool to manipulate the situation. Beware of people using this approach on you and perhaps counter by generating more options than those you have been presented with.

Remember that option generation is about finding more than one way of satisfying an interest. It is fascinating to watch some of the many television programmes where couples are helped to find a new home by some independent expert. It may be that they are looking to move out of the city or perhaps move abroad and start a new life somewhere else.

The couples tend to produce a list of requirements for the house that they hand over to the programme presenter. This list will include things like the number of bedrooms and reception rooms they want, whether the place should have a garage, land or nearby facilities such as schools. The expert will go away and find a number of properties they think meet most of the requirements. Of course, each property meets some of the requirements from each of the couples, but never all. What follows is a negotiation about the concessions that will be made by each person. They all tend to dig into positions while one of them attacks a position to elicit some kind of compromise. The husband may insist on a double garage and the wife may say, 'What do you need such a large garage for? We only have one car ...' The husband may ask, 'Why are you so insistent on such a large garden? It will require too much maintenance and you have so little time already.'

This is a classic case of each party digging into positions and each feeling that they need to make some kind of compromise for a solution to be reached. Their approach tends to be guarded and communication difficult because they both feel as though they will have to give something up if they can't get everything they really want. The result is often that neither the husband nor the wife is very happy because of the concessions they feel they have had to make. Sometimes no agreement is reached at all.

The best results usually come when the expert who acts as the third party mediator doesn't ask for requirements or positions but asks each couple about their interests. If the husband asks for a large garage, the mediator will get behind that position and ask not how big the garage needs to be, but why he needs it. It may be that the husband wants a workshop where he can pursue a hobby, or extra storage space for his tools. He or she will ask the wife not how big she wants the garden, but why she wants the garden; is it simply to look at and enjoy, to grow flowers and herbs, or an area for the kids to play safely?

This way, the third party is able to effectively separate the people from the problem and help them to go through a process that focuses upon interests and options. Perhaps a house with a separate workshop and single garage rather than a double garage will satisfy the husband. Perhaps a paved area with potted plants and herbs will satisfy the wife if what she was really interested in was growing flowers. Or a property with a park close by if she simply wanted to be amongst nature.

The key thing is that once you understand the interests of each party, you can generate a number of options that satisfy the same interest. Importantly, the mediator is not asking either party to give anything up at this stage, but is simply gathering information about their interests to gain a clearer understanding. At the end of that process the mediator will produce a list of interests and will then ask the husband and wife to comment on and criticise the list. It will include things such as storage area for tools, workshop, an area for growing flowers and herbs and access to open land and nature. Asking the couple to comment on the list of interests is much less risky and threatening than asking either of them to make concessions.

Once the list has been agreed the expert goes away and finds a number of properties that will satisfy those interests as much as possible. When the couple view the properties they are more likely to be thinking about the major issues of interest and whether these interests are being satisfied than the minutiae of the positions they would have otherwise been locked into. This way, rather than the process being a battle of wills, it becomes an exercise where they jointly explore the options they have for providing the things that are most important to them both.

Again, our social conditioning does not equip us well for generating options as we are mostly looking for single quick solutions. The best negotiators will slow the whole process down, gather as much information as possible by relentlessly pursuing the interests behind the positions and then looking for varied and creative ways of satisfying those underlying desires. It is a discipline to remain open and divergent for as long as possible rather than narrowing down early and settling on compromised agreements.

5

Using Objective Standards

*I*t is an inescapable fact that even if you have identified the other party's interests, created a state of rapport and generated creative options, that you will eventually have to agree on the price, the length of lease, delivery date or pounds per square metre. At some point you will get down to an agreement that has the figures at the bottom of the page. When it comes down to the money, you will need some way of evaluating any offer on the table. For this you will need some kind of reference point that is objective and ideally independent of both parties. This is where objective standards come in. You can manage all of the relationship issues we discussed earlier in the most constructive way possible; you can listen actively and understand the other person's point of view; you can communicate in a sensitive and caring way and acknowledge that your perception may not provide you with the fullest picture; however, none of these things should influence whether you pay one pound more or less for the product or service under negotiation. What you pay should be based upon value, measured against some criteria independent of the will or the respective power of each of the parties. A landlord may always desire to maximise his rent, and his tenants may always desire to minimise the rent, but an agreement is usually made based upon an external benchmark, in this case market value.

If you are faced with a hard positional bargainer, they will often attempt to impose their will to gain concessions from you. The skilful and consistent use of independent criteria allows you to counteract this by focusing on the problem, not the strength of the opposition. In other words, never yield because of pressure that is being applied, only to a principle that is backed up with objective evidence. When we talk about principles here, it is not about digging into a personal ideology that is in reality a positional stance. Examples abound in international relations where one nation may have ideological principles that it will insist upon being honoured only to deny the same to others; or they may attack other nations who dare to disagree with their principles. These are often positions disguised as principles. Good negotiators will always go into a negotiation having prepared the norms, the benchmarks, industry standards or list prices that are relevant to the issues they are to discuss, but at the same time will remain open to reason. We've already said that this is not about being nice; it is about being fair and doing what works. Using independent criteria will allow you to judge what is fair and help you take the journey towards what works in making agreements. Chamberlain found in 1938 that by just giving away the Sudetenland area of Czechoslovakia to Hitler, he could not appease somebody intent on pursuing his own interests regardless of others. Rewarding abusive behaviour does not work and it is important to make the distinction that negotiating with integrity is not the same as appeasement.

Consistency

However, it is important to understand that most people do have a need to be seen to be reasonable and be accepted by their peers and this need can be exploited by manipulative negotiators. Psychologically, human beings tend to look for consistency in their lives. So we look for acceptance by our peers by meeting certain social norms and standards and using these to demonstrate congruence between our words and our actions. This means that arguments are more likely to be persuasive if reference is made to behaviour or standards that are already recognised as being socially acceptable. This need for consistency is particularly powerful if tied in with core values. For example, if you are a union representative negotiating with the company regarding proposed redundancies, it is worth being very clear about the values of the organisation. If the company has declared very publicly that it is an organisation which values its employees as its major asset, then your arguments are much more persuasive if you can prove that redundancies are inconsistent with this core value. People are much more likely to want to demonstrate consistency with standards that they have already declared are important to them. This is another reason why it is important to identify the other party's values and interests during the negotiation process. However, when you negotiate with integrity, establishing this information regarding values and interests is not about using it to manipulate the other party to agree to something they don't want, but to genuinely satisfy their needs and build lasting relationships.

Be aware, however, of traps that can be set deliberately by competitive negotiators trying to manipulate. Telephone sales people use this technique. Listen carefully to the script. They will open by asking a question something like 'Would you like to save money each month on your bills?' It is clearly easy to say yes to this question, and once you have declared that as something which interests you, the sales person will go on to tell you a number of ways to achieve that. They then use arguments that are consistent with a declared interest and you will find it more difficult to find reasons to counter their proposals. Watch out for the other side attempting to get you to make agreement statements that sound fairly innocent at first. If you are negotiating the purchase of some buildings they may say,

'Do you agree that a fair way of judging the price should be by comparing recent sales in the same area?' Rather than immediately commit yourself to a principle that you may have difficulty with later on, pause, get behind the question and only agree with conditions attached. 'Well, it depends what you mean. I agree that we need to find some useful benchmarks, but they also need to reflect the location, size and condition of this property.' Agreeing to a principle with qualifiers will allow you to stay consistent with your interests at a later date if the other party springs any surprises.

Have access to authoritative standards

Before you go into any negotiation make sure you have the right people there and also that you have access to any norms or standards that you plan to refer to. If you aim to agree, either get the authority from your own organisation or ensure that the decision-maker is present. Equally, find out who is there from the other party. A tactic often used is to use some remote person who is the one you need to convince. Dr Chester Karrass is a well-known speaker on effective negotiation and he calls this technique a 'bogey'. The other side may say, 'I like the sound of your proposal, but I know my boss wouldn't go for it. He's really insistent about these things ...' Referring to some person or entity not present is a ruse. If the objective of the meeting is to agree, then the decision-makers need to be there. If they are not, then the meeting is an information-gathering exercise and not a negotiation. Be clear about the intent of the meeting and ensure that the relevant people are in attendance.

149

A variation on this tactic is the good cop/bad cop routine that we briefly mentioned earlier when discussing social similarity. If you are dealing with two people and one is being hard and the other soft, then you are probably facing a deliberate ploy. The good guy will open by talking about shared interests and common ground, therefore tapping into this concept of social similarity, where we tend to like people who see things the way we do. This will be followed by the bad guy who comes in and makes some extreme opening offer that will throw you off guard. This is designed to get you worried that agreement may be slipping away from you and to also lower your expectations.

Just as you feel that the process is starting to stall, the good guy will come back in and soften the hard proposal made by his colleague. This will demonstrate reciprocity and makes you like him even more! You may now be tempted to think about making some concessions to keep the process going and are much more likely to make concessions to the good guy, whom you feel you have some connection with. At this stage you may be so worried that the agreement hangs in the balance that your concessions may not meet your own best interests.

Be wary of such tactics employed by competitive negotiators. The way to deal with this kind of thing is to confront it head on and declare the tactic publicly in the meeting. Explain that you thought the process would be more open and straightforward and demand to know who has the authority to close. If the good guy has the authority, arrange for the bad guy to leave and get on with making the agreement.

Which standards?

The independent criteria you use will depend upon many variables. If you are buying a car, it may be the dealer's list price, comparable sales or a guide book price. The important thing is to agree the principles of how you will agree before you make the agreement. This is often a separate negotiation in itself but an important part of the process. Many industries have their own set of standards; if you are designing and purchasing a pressure vessel, in the chemical industry there are engineering norms that define the size, shape, wind loading capability, grade and thickness of material.

If there are no accepted industrial standards and a number of differing reference points, such as the car purchase above, then it may be sensible to seek some advice from somebody who knows the industry well and can demonstrate some level of independence. This person would not be helping to solve the problem or agree the price; they would simply arbitrate on the standards to be used. If you find the other party digging into a position you should try and shift the disagreement from this positional stance by having a discussion about the criteria to be used. Often this can help the relationships and the process in general as you now have a shared objective of identifying and agreeing the criteria you will use for moving the negotiation forwards.

There is also some custom and practice that is used in certain industries such as 'first in, last out' or 'first come, first served'. One approach to achieving equal treatment which children always see as fair is that of 'one cuts, the other chooses'. When one child is cutting the cake, notice the care they take in making the knife position as equitable as possible as they know their sibling will take the first slice. The other area that may be worth giving attention to is how disputes are handled. If you cannot agree, you may be able to agree how you disagree. This may mean going to arbitration or bringing in a trusted mediator who is independent of both parties. I have been in negotiations where the disputes are deferred to the CEO of each company concerned and the individuals named in the terms and conditions. Whatever standards are agreed, you must ensure that they will be applied by all parties involved.

I mentioned earlier that often positional stances can be wrapped up in declared principles. Recent examples in international relations are evident where certain factions demand freedom of expression only to violently oppose the same freedom for other countries if that expression is disagreeable to them. So make sure that you have agreed your benchmark standards, norms or criteria and also that you have explicit agreement from the other party that their behaviour will be consistent with these standards.

Authority and expertise

It is worth saying a few words about the use of experts or authority figures in negotiations, because they are often used to arbitrate or help establish standards and reference points. We are brought up in a society where we are conditioned to follow authority figures. This clearly helps a complex society manage its affairs and minimise risk while allowing people to get on with their daily business. But because we have been taught to defer to authority figures, we often disengage from our own rational and intuitive processing and run the risk of agreeing to things that are counter to our own interests. For example, in 2006 UK courts heard a case against a senior paediatrician who had acted as an expert witness in legal proceedings, upon whose testimony a number of families were split and the mothers jailed as murderers. The evidence was later found to be flawed.

From an early age our social conditioning programmes us to obey authority figures. A very interesting experiment by Stanley Milgram that began in 1961 looked at people's obedience to authority. Volunteers were asked to deliver electric shocks to other people when they made a mistake on a simple test. As the test progressed the shocks got stronger and the recipient, who was in another room, and actually an actor, was heard to react in extreme pain each time the shock was administered. Many participants continued to give shocks despite pleas for mercy from the actor, as long as the experimenter kept on ordering them to do so. This showed that people are significantly influenced by someone they perceive as an authority figure.

Another example tragically demonstrates how through desire for consistency with social standards and deference to authority figures we often override our own ability to differentiate. This is the transcript of a conversation between a pilot and co-pilot of an Air Florida flight departing from Washington D.C. on a cold, snowy day. It was reported by G. Richard Shell in his book *Bargaining for Advantage*.

(The plane is at the gate, awaiting clearance to depart. Heavy snow is falling.)

Co-pilot: See all those icicles on the back there and everything?

Captain: Yeah.

(Time passes while the plane continues to wait at the gate.)

Co-pilot: Boy, this is a, this is a losing battle here on trying to de-ice those things. It (gives) you a false feeling of security, that's all that does.

(More time passes. The snow keeps falling.)

Co-pilot: Let's check these tops (wings) again since we (have) been sitting here awhile.

Captain: I think we get to go here in a minute.

(The plane begins to taxi to the runway.)

Co-pilot: (referring to engine instrument readings): That doesn't seem right, does it? (pause.) Ah, that's not right.

Captain: Yes, it is. There's eighty (referring to an instrument).

Co-pilot: Naw, I don't think that's right. (seven-second pause) Ah, maybe it is.

Captain: Hundred and twenty.

Co-pilot: I don't know.

(The plane takes off, struggles to gain lift, and then begins to fall into the Potomac River.)

Co-pilot: Larry, we're going down, Larry.

Captain: I know it.

(Sound of impact.)

There was a government investigation following the crash in which it was found that the co-pilot was in fact correct, the instrument readings were abnormal and the flight should have been aborted. He had overcome his own doubts in the face of the authority of the captain. Sixty-nine of the 74 people on the flight, including the captain and co-pilot, died in the crash.

As with the consistency principle we talked about earlier, this basic human need can be exploited by those who understand the dynamics. I have been in complex negotiations where one or more of the parties will bring along an 'expert' in a particular field to influence the negotiation in their own favour. If the other party brings their own expert to the table, I would approach this with extreme caution. Do not accept their testimony as being true unless you have convinced yourself that the evidence exists, or test it against your own expert.

> ## Using objective standards: summary box
>
> - Get the right people there and be cautious of testimony from experts.
> - Have access to authoritative standards.
> - Negotiate about the standards early on.
> - Never yield to pressure, only principle.

Case study

Glenn Hills is a 40-bed nursing home in a town just outside Liverpool. It was built by two business partners; Simon Cutter and Danny Lloyd. Simon had some expertise in the nursing care business: he was employed as an inspector of homes in addition to owning a nursing home of his own with his wife. He was an ambitious and ruthless individual who was looking to expand his empire. Danny was an investor with little prior knowledge of the nursing sector, but he was keen to expand and share the risk of building a new home with Simon. Together they bought a piece of land and borrowed heavily from the bank to construct the new building from scratch. It was a risky time to invest, as legislation in this sector was changing and rising interest rates meant that the cost of borrowing was high. Both partners secured the loans against their personal properties.

Things went well during the construction phase; both partners were involved in monitoring progress as the purpose-built property came together piece by piece on the greenfield site. They were both also involved in testing the market for clients. They visited local hospitals, making staff aware that a new nursing home would soon be in operation, serving the local area. Because of this early marketing, once the home was built, every one of the 40 rooms was occupied within 12 months. This is an unusual and impressive result for this type of client group.

However, once there was a degree of security in the whole investment, things started to go wrong in the relationship between the partners. Simon's wife was running the home on a day-to-day basis and Simon himself, although not there as regularly, was offering advice when it was needed. Danny suggested that Simon's wife take a salary from the business, but strangely, she refused. It was only later that this seemed to be part of a broader strategy that Simon had in mind.

On the basis that they were contributing much more to the development and running of the business, Simon and his wife asked for a greater shareholding of the company that owned the nursing home. In an attempt to ease the relationship and also to reward the additional input, Danny agreed to concede some of his shareholding and passed it over to Simon and his wife.

However, things then went from bad to worse. Simon continued to feel that Danny was contributing little and demanded even more of his shareholding. Danny was increasingly frustrated with Simon's unreasonable behaviour and persistent demands for more of the business.

After nearly two years of claim and counter-claim at enormous emotional cost for the two partners and their families, the relationship broke down completely and Danny insisted that Simon buy out his shareholding. Simon was reluctant to do this as he did not want to take money from the business, so he refused.

Up until this point, the negotiations had taken place directly between the two partners. To bring the issue to a head, Danny appointed a high-profile lawyer to press his case. Protracted legal wrangling ensued as each party brought in their own legal team. As the cost of the dispute escalated, Simon eventually agreed that enough was enough and he would buy Danny out of the partnership.

The negotiation now became a matter of agreeing the value of Danny's shareholding. Simon's initial offer was based upon Danny's share of the current value of the building and the land only; in other words, the value of the material assets. Furthermore, he had calculated this using only the current equity in the home: the market value minus the borrowings still owed to the banks. As the business was still in its early stages and a significant amount of the loan was still outstanding, this figure was very small. Danny refused this first offer, knowing he could do better.

Simon's team continued to insist that the valuation be based upon the bricks and mortar value of the building and of the surrounding land. To his despair, Danny's advisors initially agreed with the analysis of Simon's team. Danny was confused because he knew this did not take into account anything related to the performance of the business itself, which by now was well established and making a significant annual profit. In the same way that a car can be valued in a number of different ways — comparative prices, book value, adjustments for mileage or condition — Danny knew that the complex matter of a business must be subject to a number of different valuation methods. He refused the offer made by Simon's team. The protracted negotiations had now gone on for nearly three years and legal costs were continuing to mount.

The deadlock was finally broken by both sides agreeing to put the matter to an independent arbitrator. A large accounting firm was appointed to look at the case and rule on the valuation of the shareholding. Each party was able to present a case for the arbitration through their respective legal teams and each partner signed an agreement stating that they would abide by the decision of the arbitrator; Simon Cutter was confident that the valuation would be based upon the material value of the assets; Danny Lloyd still wanted the valuation to be broader than this.

After some investigation, Danny did find a method that took into account the performance of the business. This was related to the current turnover as well as the predicted earnings over a period of ten years. He built his petition around this — his valuation was at least three times the figure produced by the other valuation method. Predictably, Simon was outraged. When he heard, he made an angry visit to the arbitrator in the accounting firm's offices to tell him what he thought of the valuation. The arbitrator was disgusted and threw him out of his office.

Simon had now undermined the impartiality of the process, leaving the arbitrators with a problem which was eventually solved by using a different individual from the same large company, but from a different city. Each party agreed to the change. The valuation eventually fell with Danny's method of calculation and a substantial payment was made from Glenn Hills Nursing Home. Simon was so upset at the ruling that he tried to take the firm of accountants that acted as arbitrators to court. That case still continues ...

Analysis

Apart from the message that you should choose your business partners carefully, there are a number of points to be noted in this case.

The best negotiations provide clarity at the implementation stage. Although in this case each partner was bringing something different to the arrangement, those things should have been openly declared and agreed before they proceeded. Simon Cutter clearly brought technical expertise in the nursing home sector that Danny did not possess, but Simon could not raise the funds on his own and needed Danny's investment to make the project happen. If anyone thought that the difference in their contributions should affect the 50/50 split of the shareholding, they should have agreed this in the first place. This was assumed rather than negotiated and was the source of Simon Cutter's original feelings of inequity.

Danny Lloyd yielded to the pressure applied by Simon rather than basing his response on the principles that had been agreed at the outset. We said earlier that you should never yield to pressure, only to principle. One party growing unhappy with the balance of contribution later on in the project does not necessarily undermine the original principles. The contribution by Simon's wife could have been rewarded in other ways, such as insisting that she take the salary that was offered. It could be that, right from the beginning, Simon harboured a strategy that included eventually driving out his partner. Even if this were the case, being clear about the principles of the original agreement and how each contribution was rewarded should have been enough for Danny to resist the pressure regardless of how aggrieved Simon felt. If there was genuine imbalance, then some criteria independent of the will of both parties should have been used to determine this, not the force of pressure applied by one party.

Nobody wants to be in a partnership where there is discontent. However, as we stated earlier, rewarding abusive behaviour with concessions does not provide lasting solutions. Just as Chamberlain found that he could not appease Hitler with a little bit of Czechoslovakia, even when Danny conceded some of his shareholding, Simon wanted more.

Whether you are in a healthy relationship or one with somebody who insists on pursuing their own interests at the expense of yours, you need some way of measuring value and fairness. This example shows that the determination of the standards to be used is not always straightforward. There are often a number of ways of establishing the reference points you need and the methods of doing this should be considered carefully.

Be wary of the advice of experts; they often don't agree with each other. It is better to keep your own counsel as much as you can; listen most carefully to your own intuition, which will be heightened by researching and speaking to a lot of different people as a way of getting a feel for the subject area. This way, you put yourself in a position of total responsibility. If Danny Lloyd had listened only to his first expert advisor, he would have been out of pocket by several hundred thousand pounds.

The skilful use of independent criteria again separates the people issues from the problem itself. It helps agreements to be made based upon what is fair rather than what one party wants. Simon wanted to pay much less for the shareholding, but what he actually paid in the end was determined by reference to an objective standard which was related to value and fairness.

The practice

6

Planning and Preparation

The foundation to successful negotiation lies in planning an effective strategy. Let's now pull together some of the concepts we have discussed up to this point. The diagram on the next page illustrates the elements that are to be managed to navigate successfully towards agreement.

When you plan a strategy for a negotiation, you are actually preparing to go through a number of distinct stages: gathering and sharing information, generating options, making offers and concessions, and closing. Most transactions we undertake tend to pass through these stages, even though we may not be consciously aware of the distinctions. When you go along to a

Generating options (Chapter 4)

- Establish a creative environment for generating options
- If a menu of choices doesn't exist, create one
- Expand the pie before you cut it
- Consider brainstorming with the other side

Making offers and concessions

- Use objective standards to establish fairness (Chapter 5)
- Have the right people and be cautious of testimony from experts
- Get access to authoritative standards
- Negotiate about the standards early
- Identify your best alternatives

Closure and implementation

- Have an implementation strategy
- Review progress

Planning and preparation

* Be clear what you want
* Put yourself in their shoes
* Know your alternatives
* Build relationships

Personal preparation

* Get into a peak state
* Visualise your outcomes

Gathering and sharing information: Focus on values and interests
(Chapter 1)

* Get behind positions to identify underlying needs
* Know your own style and understand your personal values and interests
* Use questions to build understanding and trust
* Prioritise multiple interests

Gathering and sharing information: Communication
(Chapters 2 and 3)

* Communicate to understand and be understood
* Separate the people issues from the substance of the negotiation
* Be aware of how your perceptions can be influenced and never yield to pressure, only to reason
* Be creative, not reactive; take the initiative and set the tone for the negotiation
* Deal with the emotions

restaurant for example, you signal your interest in ordering by sitting down and asking the waiter for the menu to see what is on offer (gathering and sharing information). You may actually ask if there are any specials on that don't appear on the menu (generating options) and then perhaps have a discussion about whether you can have the salad instead of the chips with the fish (making offers and concessions). The waiter may have to check with the kitchen whether it is possible to make the change, but once he has confirmed, you put in your order (closing).

It is clearly a much more complex process when undertaking a negotiation, but the same distinct steps must be navigated. Notice how the things we have already discussed fit into this overall model. The gathering and sharing of information is addressed under values and interests (Chapter 1), communication (Chapter 2) and managing perceptions (Chapter 3). Generating options (Chapter 4) is followed by objective criteria (Chapter 5), which is the key process for measuring whether any offers of concessions are fair and equitable.

In more complex situations the process may be repeated a number of times. For example, if no closure is reached following the offer and concession stage, then the parties may go back to option generation or information sharing. The amount of time spent in each of these stages varies from person to person and from deal to deal. It may also differ according to the participants' background and culture. The eastern approach to negotiation, such as that taken in China, seems to spend more time on the planning, information sharing and option generation stages before they move quickly and efficiently through the offer-making and concession stage. In the west, we tend to like to move quickly to making offers and concessions and reach closure by thrashing things out at this stage.

However the stages are managed, skilled negotiators tend to know where they are in the process even when it is not neat and linear. It is therefore important to actively manage each stage. If the information gathering stage is overlooked, then it will have an effect on the quality of the later stages and ultimately the final agreement, if one is reached. That's a little like ordering at the restaurant without looking at the menu properly and then complaining when the next table get something that looks much better than your order. You may recall that Rackham and Carlisle noticed how the skilled group of negotiators spent twice as much time as the average group gathering information during the negotiation process. Effectively managing each of the stages requires a planning strategy.

Let us now have a look at some of the things that can be done during the planning and preparation phase of any negotiation. Negotiating with integrity is as much to do with the attitude of mind you bring into the negotiating room with you as with the application of the tools and techniques described here (although both are important to optimise your results). I find that the best outcomes are achieved by giving attention to both the personal and practical elements of preparation during the planning phase. In this chapter we will look at both the strategic and personal planning that can be done to help get the most from your bargaining experiences. The strategic planning includes those practical and material elements of the preparation, such as assessing your alternatives, establishing clarity of purpose and preparing the environment. The strategic planning can also include those things that can be done well in advance of the actual negotiation. The personal planning is about getting yourself in the right frame of mind before you enter the negotiation and is something usually best done just before you enter the room. The most effective plan will be one that has a strategy for each of the stages in the model as well as an idea of how you are to optimise your own personal resources.

Strategic planning

This is all about being clear about your own values and interests and being focused on what you want, not what you don't. Consider using the proforma on the next page to guide your preparation and start by listing your goals and desired outcomes.

Be clear what you want

However, it is important to make a definition between having goals and establishing a bottom line. A bottom line is the minimum point at which you are able to say yes to the other party, the point below which you walk away because you are able to achieve more by not negotiating or waiting for the next opportunity. A positive bargaining zone is created if the two parties negotiating have bottom lines that allow for agreement to take place. For example, if you are selling a car and your bottom line is £2000 and an interested buyer has a bottom line of £2500, which is the maximum they will pay for a car of your specification, there is a positive bargaining zone of £500. It is referred to as a negative bargaining zone if the bottom lines do not overlap.

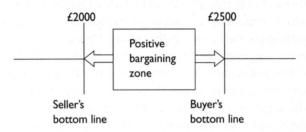

Having a bottom line gives you a sense of clarity and certainty and also provides a trigger point for saying no. However, a bottom line is also a position around which the focus of your negotiation could be pivoted. What this means is that often when things become complicated in negotiations the tendency is to focus upon the things that have been fixed. In our example of the car seller above, if he fixes a bottom line at £2000, he is likely to relax and perhaps stop the bargaining process if the buyer offers him anything above £2000.

Setting goals is different. A goal is a realistic target where expectations are set by using some objective standard. In the case of our car seller, it could be by comparing prices in local garages or ads. Our seller therefore may set a goal of £2300 using this external standard. This will completely shift his focus and help him achieve a better price. His £2000 bottom line may be based upon some other standard such as the amount he needs to repay his finance, but by focusing on his goals rather than his bottom line he may be much more successful in his negotiation. Considering that the buyer will probably be focused on his bottom line (£2500) then a much better deal for the seller is likely to be made. You get what you focus on, so avoid your focus being on your bottom line; which is the minimum level acceptable to you.

In the Rackham and Carlisle research which compared the behaviour of skilled and average negotiators they found that when it came to setting limits for the negotiation, the group of average performers tended to plan for a fixed point objective. The skilled group were more likely to plan in terms of a range, with upper, target and lower points, and were more likely to go into the negotiation with a package of options that would meet their needs. This brings us back once more to understanding your values and interests and entering the negotiation with a range of options, based upon independent criteria that will satisfy both your own and those of the other party. So, during the preparation phase, being clear about your own needs is of primary importance.

When setting goals and establishing bottom lines, it is easy to forget that the more qualitative elements are often more important than the figures. The objective is to satisfy your interests, which is not always about securing a victory on the price. If you are purchasing a car, the size, comfort of drive, mileage, condition or even colour may form your primary interests; then you can start negotiating the price. If approached as a competition about how much you pay, it is all too easy to win the battle on price but end up with a car that doesn't meet your needs. Being clear about what you are trying to accomplish beforehand helps to avoid getting caught up in the competitive issues once the negotiation has started and the pressure is on.

Again looking at some of the evidence from Rackham and Carlisle's research, they found that both the skilled and the average group of negotiators spent time on planning, but it was the areas that they focused on which made the biggest difference to the outcomes. Both groups spent most of their planning time looking at satisfying their own values and interests; however, the skilled group spent twice as much time as the average group exploring options which the other party may introduce and more than three times as much looking for areas of common ground between the parties. Overall, this skilled group spent nearly four times more of their planning time, 40% in total, on issues relating to the other party's interests, joint options or areas of common ground.

The following preparation sheet will help to clarify your thinking during the preparation. Start by working through your own thinking — interests, alternatives, options, etc. — and then put yourself in the position of the other party and complete the same boxes looking at the negotiation from their point of view. This will allow you to spot areas of common ground, potential issues and perhaps options that will satisfy theirs as well as your interests. Also make reference to any objective criteria that you think is relevant and bring the details along to the negotiation.

Negotiation preparation sheet

	Ours	The other party
Background and perceptions		
Negotiable issues		
Challenges or obstacles		
Values and interests		
Alternatives		
Options		
Priorities		
Strategy		
Objective criteria		
First meeting planning		

Know your alternatives

The only reason that we negotiate is to get a better outcome than by not negotiating at all. You will only ever agree with the other party if what they are offering is better than your alternatives. Considered in this way, if you have a clear alternative each time you go into any negotiation, you can make every negotiation a success because you will always secure the best deal available to you. This means that part of your preparation should include clearly identifying your alternatives to reaching agreement. This gives another reference point for judging the favourability of proposals made by the other side. You may well enter a negotiation with a clear bottom line and your goals, but you should also compare any proposals made with your alternatives to see if it better satisfies your needs.

Fisher and Ury in their book *Getting to Yes* describe this concept as having a BATNA: a best alternative to a negotiated agreement. Knowing your BATNA gives you a sense of clarity in any negotiation. But that clarity comes only from having a realistic and balanced view of your alternatives. Retailers will often try to cultivate a limited perception of your alternatives when they offer items for sale for a limited time only. You may panic and buy based upon this perception, when in actual fact there may be another sale in a month's time, you may get a similar product from a different supplier or decide not to purchase at all. It is a little like rushing for a train when you are late and risking life and limb to arrive before it leaves. Your perception of the situation at the time makes it feel very important to get that train; however, you may be able to take the next train, travel by car, conduct your meeting over the phone or make arrangements to meet tomorrow. On the other side of the same argument, it is easy to have an over-optimistic view of your alternatives. I once held out for the best price on a house I was selling only to end up waiting nearly two years to sell the property. If I had assessed the market better and had a clearer view of the alternatives available as well as my primary interests at the time, I may have sold for less, but much earlier, which would have been much more financially beneficial.

The other common pitfall is to be seduced by the cumulative attraction of the alternatives you feel you have. If you don't agree on this job, you may feel that there are many other things you can do; you could start your own business, write that book you've been thinking about or move to another part of the country. The list may sound very attractive, but remember that you must choose only one of these options, you cannot do them all. This is why it is called a best alternative; you must assess those options you have and be disciplined enough to choose the one that best fits your needs.

So, don't be tempted to go into the negotiation thinking, 'I'll see what the other party offers and then think about my alternatives.' Having a BATNA will give you a clear reference point with which to measure the value of any proposals. Having a strong BATNA gives you power, even when the perception is that the other party have the advantage.

I observed a negotiation in a shoe shop recently where a customer wanted to buy a pair of boots. The customer picked a pair of boots and told the manager that he could get exactly the same pair £10 cheaper at a rival shop in another part of the town. The manager clearly wanted the sale and started to reduce the price incrementally. It was also clear, however, that the customer had done his homework and knew he had a viable alternative. He didn't flinch at the manager's continued offers because he knew exactly what his alternative was and of course the manager knew this too. The customer stated that he was willing to go back to the other shop, but he was here and willing to buy now if the price was matched. If he had accepted the small incremental reductions, it may have looked like a bluff and the reaction of the manager may have been different.

We often feel that the other party has the power, particularly in a situation like this where the shop seems to hold the advantage. Because he was crystal clear about his alternatives the power in the negotiation shifted in the favour of the customer and he walked away with the boots at the price he had requested.

Of course it is not always possible to enter a negotiation with a powerful alternative. But neither is it helpful to fall into the thinking that the only solution lies with the other party; good alternatives are actively generated through good strategic preparation. It is most common for people to commit too early because they see their only solution being an agreement at the negotiating table when the best outcome may lie elsewhere. Thinking that your only options are those you can negotiate with the other party will limit thinking and creativity. Preparing a realistic view of your alternatives before you enter any negotiation will give you this clarity. A little like the brainstorming process described earlier, list your alternatives and fortify those that you think are most attractive. It may mean sourcing other suppliers or even applying for other jobs if a new job or salary increase is what you are negotiating. Imagine going into a salary negotiation with another job offer on the table and see how that affects your attitude and perceived power. The strongest of the alternatives that you create is your BATNA. So, don't fall into the trap of thinking you have no other alternatives, but remember they must be identified or even created as part of your preparation strategy.

Just as we talked earlier about putting yourself in the other party's shoes to identify their values and interests, the same approach should be taken to attempt to identify their alternatives. It is all too easy to perceive the other party as being more powerful than you, but don't make this assumption without doing some work to find out what their BATNA may be. If the other side really is more powerful, then negotiating with integrity works well for you as you should keep pulling the negotiation away from the power and towards the principles.

Negotiating with integrity does not necessarily mean that you disclose all of your information at once to the other party as that may not be in your best interests. So, whether you disclose your BATNA depends upon the circumstances. If you have a weak alternative, there is no reason to declare this and focus on your weaknesses. Focus on your strengths and keep pulling the line of thinking towards the principles of satisfying interests, generating mutually acceptable options and using objective criteria. On the other hand, if you do go into a salary negotiation and have another offer on the table, you should almost certainly be honest about this rather than use it as a deliberate manipulation tool. Like the customer in the shoe shop, declaring his alternative at the outset and stating his intentions gave him the best foundation for satisfying his interests.

Build relationships

Negotiators are human beings before anything else and managing the relationship you have with the other side is the area that will determine success or failure more than any other. We've already discussed communication skills and the importance of building rapport. We also found that people are more likely to buy from you if they like you and are like you, as well as agreement being much more likely to occur if people are understood. These are all factors associated with building relationships. In my experience many deals are often done before you get into the negotiation room. This is particularly the case in those complicated deals where a large number of people may be involved. Often the key players will get together and thrash out the main issues together and bring their conclusions back to the table. But this is not about being friends; it is about finding a balance in the working relationship that gives both parties what they want. There is some research that indicates that people in close relationships are much more likely to be 'soft' in their bargaining approach and make equal compromises. Three professors conducted a bargaining study designed to observe the bargaining behaviour for the purchase and resale of three different appliances. The people used in the study, who were to negotiate with each other, were 74 dating couples and 32 pairs of men and women who were strangers. The study found that the dating couples tended to avoid conflict more, so argued less; they set less aggressive goals and gave more concessions, tending to reach agreement through compromise. The strangers were much more likely to look for creative options, set more ambitious targets and actively explore interests and priorities.

As with the sisters and the orange, compromising doesn't always give you the best solution. Skilful negotiators are concerned with being fair, but they are also very assertive about their values and interests being satisfied and will challenge the other party to move away from simple compromises and towards finding the best solutions for everybody concerned. Cultivating this kind of relationship with the key players on the other side should form part of your preparation strategy. If you can, make this connection with them before the negotiations begin, away from the office, over a meal, or on the golf course. If that opportunity is not available, at least try to meet them before you start your negotiations; arrive early and make a point of making some kind of contact and connection with them to establish your approach. Principles such as social similarity and reciprocity are powerful magnetising forces in human communication. Even though I am aware of these principles, I am always more socially drawn to those who approach me with an area of common interest or a story that directly relates to my own understanding. Once that connection is made, communication is always much more fluent. Identifying the decision-makers and building some kind of rapport with them in order to cultivate a sense of mutual respect and understanding will reap benefits in all of your negotiations.

Personal preparation

There's a wonderful quote from Mahatma Gandhi who said, 'I've got so much to do today that I'll have to meditate for twice as long.' Your success in your negotiations will be a reflection of the quality of your personal and environmental preparation.

Get into a 'peak state'

I've consistently found that the state of mind you are in when you enter any interaction is a powerful factor in determining the results that you get. Whatever you sincerely desire and believe that it is possible for you to attain, will eventually manifest in your life. Your own expectations are something that are within your control and should form part of your preparation before you enter any negotiation. There is a great story about Elvis Presley: wherever he was performing he would have his trailer placed one thousand paces from the venue. Whatever frame of mind he was in when he left the trailer, by the time he had taken his thousand steps to the venue, he was in such a powerful state of mind that his presence and performance on stage would induce a tangible frenzy of excitement in the audience. Your most powerful and resourceful state is your peak state. This is not about turning you into something that you are not; it is about creating a state of mind that allows you to be so naturally yourself that you are able to access all of the rational and intuitive skills which are inherently within you. Many people get so nervous or are so profoundly influenced by external circumstances that they are seldom able to perform at their optimum. Getting into a peak state allows you access to this space.

Try the following exercise and observe if it allows you to spontaneously create a greater feeling of resourcefulness.

Getting into your peak state

1. Find yourself a quiet area where you will not be disturbed. While standing, take a deep breath and as you breathe out, close your eyes. Feel yourself relaxed but still alert.

2. If you feel a sense of nervousness before you go into the negotiation, tune into the physical sensations that you are creating in your body. Identify where you feel the reaction to your

nervous state of mind; it is often a light 'fluttering' sensation in the throat or heart region. Imagine drawing this energy down the body into the abdominal region so that it sits behind your solar plexus. When this energy is drawn down, feel the sense of being grounded that it brings. Feel that connection through the soles of the feet as if you are powerfully rooted to the spot. The feeling should give you a sensation of stability that flows through your soles into the earth beneath you. Imagine that you radiate this presence through your body and have the tangible focus and stability of a powerful animal like a bull. Focus on that feeling of being powerful and stable for a few seconds.

3. With your eyes still closed, imagine that there is a circle drawn on the ground in front of you. Give it a positive, strong colour.

4. Think of an experience in your life where everything went spectacularly well for you. It doesn't have to be associated with performance at work, it could be in any area of your life where you felt confident, in control and things worked out exactly as you wanted them. The feelings this example generates are more important than the circumstances. If you really can't find a strong enough example, identify a role model in your life who really embodies the qualities you want to emulate.

5. With your eyes still closed, step into the imaginary circle on the ground in front of you. When you step into the circle, you also step into the experience that you have recalled, or if it is a role model, see yourself step into their body.

6. As you step into the circle, use all of your senses to re-live the experience. Imagine feeling the things that you felt at the time, see the things that you saw and hear the things that were said. Really take yourself back to the experience (or if you are using a role model; imagine how they would deal with any challenges; what would they feel, say, do, think?).

7. Once you get into this mental state, hold yourself there and then double the sensations that you are having, so that you feel a sense of pulsing confidence surging through your body.

8. Once you are experiencing the most profound level of experience you can, press the thumb and middle finger of the right hand together tightly. When you do this you anchor a connection between the state of mind you are in and the physical gesture. This is a trigger.

9. Repeat the exercise until whenever you create the trigger on your right hand you bring yourself to the state of mind you have induced. This is your peak state.

The other aspect of being in a peak state for successful negotiations is the management of your own energetic resources. You cannot perform at your peak level intellectually or mentally if you are not in good physical shape. Think about doing some simple mobility movements before you go into any important meeting and notice how it frees you up physically as well as mentally. Drink plenty of water and if you are conducting negotiations over lunch or dinner, eat light and do not drink any alcohol so that you remain alert and focused.

The negotiations held during the takeover of MG Rover by the Chinese car company Nanjing can illustrate. Observers during the protracted negotiations noted that the MG Rover representatives were plied with wine over many meal-time bargaining sessions. The Chinese contingent kept their glasses filled but never drank and so remained sober throughout. Many of the agreements left the union and managers unhappy and led Geoffrey Robinson, Labour MP for Coventry North West and former Jaguar boss to remark to the BBC that the deal 'seems fraught with difficulties'. See your mental and energetic resources as part of your responsibility in the negotiation process and manage them actively and consciously.

Visualise your outcomes

Getting yourself into this peak state before you go into any negotiation will help you to access the most resourceful state that you are capable of. Implicit within the definition of negotiating with integrity is a need for us all to be consistent with our most fundamental values in our personal and professional dealings. In short this means that you need to be yourself as much as you can in negotiations but use some of the tools and techniques that have been described here to express yourself in the most clear and articulate way possible. This is not about you attempting to contort yourself into behaving in ways that are not consistent with your values just to get better results. The best and most satisfying results will be those that are attained when you feel you have been true to yourself and the things that you value the most. Another technique that may help bring you closer to this level of self-expression is to visualise the outcomes that you desire. Try the following exercise, even if you have never done anything like this before.

Visualisation exercise

1. Do this as you are finishing off your peak state exercise. While still standing in the circle, take your mind from the past positive experience and project your thoughts into the future; into the negotiation you are about to undertake.

2. See yourself staying in touch with your personal needs and values and being able to express those things with ease and confidence, regardless of any other external factors.

3. See and feel the flow of communication occurring naturally and effortlessly and feel a profound sense of satisfaction as you stay in control of your own strategy and true to your own values.

4. See the most positive outcome possible taking place. It is important that this is a harmonious picture, not only that your interests are met, but also that the other party is happy with the outcome. At some level, your unconscious will show resistance to imagery that includes the other party being manipulated, cajoled or pressured against their will.

5. Dwell for a while in the feelings created by this picture and see the conclusion of your meeting; everyone shaking hands, celebrating the result and leaving feeling happy with the outcome.

6. Once complete, step forward out of the circle as you open your eyes and back to a normal state of consciousness. See this as being symbolic of your stepping forward into the future and taking with you the imagery and state of mind that you have just experienced.

7. As you step into the negotiation room use your trigger and step into the state you have just created.

Planning and preparation: summary box

- Plan and prepare for each stage of the negotiation process (complete the preparation sheet in this chapter).
- Be clear about what you want to achieve.
- Be clear about your alternatives.
- Pre-pave the way to the negotiation room by cultivating positive relationships.
- Get yourself into the optimum physical and mental state before you begin negotiating.

7

Closure and Implementation

As with any sale, the crucial moment is the one of closure and commitment. Many agreements made at the negotiation table have unravelled once the parties leave. This is because there is a difference between agreement and commitment. This is summed up nicely with the well-known adage regarding the role of the hen and the pig in a bacon and egg breakfast. While the hen is only involved in the breakfast, the pig is definitely committed! Once you get an agreement at the negotiating table, you need to ensure that you secure some form of commitment to the deal. Real commitment involves tangible risk and can often only be secured by setting up the agreement so that if anyone pulls out, each party has something to lose. When we touched upon commitment in Chapter 3, we talked about the consistency principle and the fact that if people commit to something, particularly if it is a public commitment, then they generally feel the need to follow through.

Commitment takes many forms in different circumstances: a handshake in certain social groups may be enough to seal commitment; with other deals it may be a public announcement, a down-payment or the signing of a written agreement. Notice that if you ask somebody to a barbeque without obligation, they often don't bother turning up. If you ask them to come and bring along dessert, and explain that the other guests will contribute to another course, they are much more likely to arrive. This is because they feel a sense of commitment to the project and feel that if they don't turn up then dessert will definitely be missed and they risk other people judging that they have not been consistent to their promise.

Closure and commitment is an important and tense time and you should be on the lookout for some of the tactics that we mentioned earlier. For example, we discussed scarcity, which can be deliberately cultivated to elicit early closure from you or concessions that you otherwise would not have made. I remember when I was a teenager selling my first car and having advertised it for a number of weeks without any response. I was thinking of dropping the price when I got two calls on the same day from interested parties. I arranged for the second party to arrive while the first was still there and ended up getting slightly more than my asking price because the two parties ended up haggling on my front drive over a car they thought was in great demand.

The important thing is to get the closure and commitment and then to have a plan for making sure that each party plays its part in the detail of the implementation. It is easy in the heat of the negotiation process to forget that you need to have a plan for turning your agreements into performance.

Research shows that skilled negotiators are very concerned about implementation planning and will get the snags sorted out as part of the negotiation process before the main parties leave. This is a lot less painful than hitting problems later on which will potentially damage relationships and perhaps affect performance. Get explicit commitment from all parties involved and agree an implementation strategy while the decision-makers are there to endorse it.

Power and leverage

Often you will find yourself in a situation where the other side is more powerful than you; they may have more money, firepower, time or people. In situations like this it is important to ensure that you have taken steps to protect yourself by not making agreements that will harm your interests. This means being very clear about your alternatives and having identified and strengthened your BATNA as we discussed in the previous chapter. If your best alternative is to make an agreement with the party you are negotiating with, you need then to ensure that you make the most of the assets you have. However, even when it seems that the other party has all of the power it does not automatically follow that they will have everything their own way. Even when the other side is more powerful, you can strengthen your own position if you have leverage.

Power and leverage are different things. Donald Trump once described leverage as 'having something the other guy wants. Or better yet, needs. Or best of all, simply cannot do without.' This is why sports people or entertainers are often able to negotiate huge salaries when dealing with immensely powerful corporations. The individuals may have an image, a talent or an existing fan base that gives them enormous leverage to get what they want even from seemingly powerful organisations. The organisations also know that the individuals have very strong alternatives, so if they don't agree, there is almost certainly another interested party waiting in the wings to sign them up.

An obvious and disturbing use of leverage is demonstrated by hostage-takers and terrorists who, by taking captives or making threats of violence will demand the attention of even the most powerful of military forces. Al Capone, the American gangster is said to have remarked, 'You can get much further with a kind word and a gun than you can with a kind word alone.' Before you assume that the other party has all the power, assess your own resources and see if you have anything that can be used as leverage. The chances are that you do have something that the other party wants or needs otherwise they would not be negotiating in the first place. Also, strengthen your position as much as you can. Assess, and if necessary develop your alternatives; it's a little like going into the job interview we mentioned earlier with another offer on the table. This will make you feel significantly better about pursuing your own interests even in the face of seemingly powerful opposition. If you have done all this and still feel significantly out-gunned, then keep bringing the discussions back to principles and interests. Talk about your emotions and how you feel you have a right to have your interests satisfied. Even the most competitive positional bargainers will listen hard if they feel they have something to lose. Establish the style of the other party by looking at graph showing the negotiation styles at the beginning of this book.

When we discussed these different approaches to negotiation we said that positional bargainers will often have a high concern for satisfying their own interests and a low concern for yours. If this is the case, you may need to influence their perception so that they move a little further up the scale that demonstrates concern for other people.

For example, earlier we described a real project where the residents clashed with the development company who were transporting materials through a residential area to construct a new railway station. The residents' spokesperson built some rapport with the construction manager by demonstrating an understanding of his interests, but at the same time needed to change his perceptions and raise his concerns about the residents' interests. When she said, *'I've already explained that we fully understand the commercial pressures you are under and the benefits we will all get from the completed project, but surely you are not saying that those things are more important than the safety of our children?'* she was sliding him up the 'concern for others' scale and also pointing out that ignoring the residents' interests could be painful; the last thing that any organisation wants is non-co-operation of locals or a bad press. Finding these areas of leverage is key to managing parties that are more powerful.

How the other party views their own power depends to an extent on how they see their relationship with you. Seeing the agreement as a one-off transaction will lead them to take a short-term view, keeping the power to themselves. Decisions will probably be based primarily on price, delivery etc. and other factors will be seen as secondary. If on the other hand they see your relationship as part of an ongoing partnership then they may see price as being only one of a number of variables that affect the way the agreement is made. Things like market share or public image may also impact on the way they wish to share the power with you and the way they see their relationship with you in the much longer term.

Those who aim to keep power, at the top of the graph opposite, are those positional bargainers who wish to win regardless of the other party's interests and stay in control of the process. Those at the bottom are willing to share the power and create 'I win, you win' solutions. They tend to see themselves as problem-solvers and see the benefits in satisfying the interests of

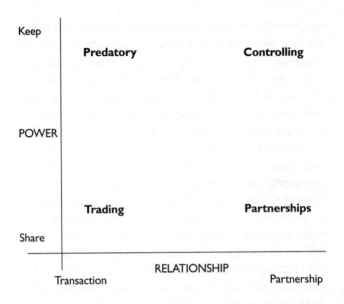

the other party to create mutually beneficial solutions. It is clearly easier to negotiate with parties that are in the same sector as you in this graph, but understanding their position will at least allow you to identify their strategy.

Negotiating in different cultures

Different countries approach negotiation with reference to the predominant mode in that culture. Those who are willing to share the power and are transaction-orientated are traders, barterers and hagglers. Even if the transactions are one-offs and the parties unlikely to deal again, there is a commitment to each party profiting, and compromise and concession are elements

of the transactions. This mode is seen in countries of
the Middle East and Africa. Where bartering is the
predominant mode, there is an expectation that
the process will be approached in a particular way.
Often you are expected to come in with a high offer
and there will be a series of concessions from each
party that will converge on the value of the goods or
service. There is a scene in the Monty Python film *Life
of Brian* where one character wants to buy an item from
a market trader very quickly. He asks the trader how
much he wants and gives him the amount equal to his
opening offer. The trader is deeply offended that they
have not gone through the ritual of haggling and
follows him down the street. This is not a recommend-
ation that you get drawn into the strategy of the other
party, but a flag to raise awareness that there are
sometimes certain social expectations about how the
process of agreeing is approached.

Those who wish to keep the power and are transaction-orientated do not tend to bargain, but will buy
and sell on the basis of a fixed price, or on a take-it-or-
leave-it or let-the-market-fix-the-price basis. This is a
mode predominant in North America. Many western
countries tend to be very results-orientated and often
move very quickly through the gathering and sharing
information and option-generation phases of negotiations. They want to quickly get to the stage where
opening offers are made and proposals and concessions are debated.

Those who wish to control the power but are committed to a long-term relationship tend to be those

organisations that dominate their market, such as monopolies or governments. This approach tends to predominate in Japan. Often eastern cultures do tend to be much more relationship driven and will spend a great deal of time gathering information as well as building trust and understanding between the parties. This can mean that the offer and concession stage of the negotiation takes place quickly and efficiently.

Partners are in a long-term relationship but on more equal terms than controllers. They will be flexible on price in order to maintain this equilibrium and tend to believe in customer or brand loyalty. They see a transaction as part of a relationship and are willing to co-operate at all stages of negotiation and implementation as equals. This is the dominant mode in Sweden.

Keep	**USA**				
					Japan
			France		
		China			
			Russia		
POWER			**Germany**		
		UK			
	Italy				
					Sweden
Share	**Middle East**				

RELATIONSHIP

Transaction — Partnership

Although this is a generalisation based upon anecdotal evidence, it allows you to be aware of the differing approaches in different cultures and again be on your guard to adjust your style according to the other party's approach and the strategy they are used to dealing with. However, I would put less importance on cultural, or gender stereotypes for that matter, and more on the things that you observe and interpret using your own senses when interacting with people across the table. By all means use the information to avoid insensitive blunders; definitely take the time to learn if there are gestures, phrases or approaches that could cause offence; however, your most effective results will come from good communication and effective rapport-building with other human beings.

Using emotional Aikido

What if the other party refuses to play the game of principled negotiation and digs into a position they will not budge from? What if they start to attack you personally or use dirty tricks to meet their own interests? Observation of nature demonstrates that you get an equal and opposite reaction to any applied force. Also, what you resist, persists! In other words if you are pushed and you push back, you will get into a cycle of resistance that will expend lots of energy but not necessarily get you any further towards making an agreement.

There is a martial art called Aikido which is essentially a defensive use of movement and energy that teaches how to deflect an opponent's attack and use the energy created to your advantage. In negotiations, if you are attacked by the other side, do not react. Your reaction will create the momentum for the cycle to perpetuate and you will be drawn into the game the other party is playing.

Rather than counter the attack, attempt to deflect it in another direction. For example if you are attacked personally, reframe the statement as an attack on the problem. If you are criticised, simply listen to what is said and actually invite further comments on your behaviour or proposals, asking how they could be improved. Don't take these things personally; what people say and do is more a reflection of what they think about themselves than what they think of you. Remember that other people see things through the lens of their own perception, and listening to their statements will give you more information about their position, interests and values. If it does feel like a personal attack, the other party is probably trying to satisfy a need in the only way they currently know. Always be looking behind their position and dig a little deeper if necessary to understand the interest they are trying to satisfy. This is a prime opportunity for practising the question-asking skills we described earlier.

Often, making statements, particularly if they are stated as facts from your perspective, will generate resistance, whereas asking questions will help to gather information. Once you have asked the question, stay silent. Silences are very uncomfortable, particularly during tense negotiations, but this means that somebody will feel compelled to fill the void. You may find that absorbing the responses you get will be enough to take the energy from the situation and provide you with a basis for building rapport. Again, listening carefully to the other party's comments and asking them to elaborate, clarify or offer suggestions as to how you could improve your proposals does not imply agreement with their position, it simply shows an attempt to understand the whole situation better. The most successful Aikido masters are those who stick to their own game plan and refuse to be drawn into playing by the rules of their opponent.

So, in a negotiation, the important thing is to not be reactive, but to break the cycle of attack and refuse to be drawn into the other party's tactics. If they continue with the positional stance, get behind the position by asking why. Why that particular number? What is it based upon and what was the process that helped you to arrive at it? Identify the interests that underlie the position and make suggestions that could also satisfy the interest. Ask them to explain your position, so that they understand your interests and allow them to fully understand the consequences of their position. If they aren't already aware of it, get them to understand their BATNA and explain what your alternatives are.

These things will help to get behind the attack or the position and redirect it towards something more constructive. At the same time, allow the other party the opportunity to come back, or climb down without losing face. As William Ury says in *Getting Past No*: 'Build them a golden bridge.'

Review your own performance
As human beings, we tend to learn by having an experience, analysing our performance afterwards and

then making adjustments to our behaviour next time. This review process is a good life-skill to develop and will definitely help to deepen your skills as a negotiator. Actively look for opportunities to practise some of the techniques and principles described in this book, and if the relationship allows it, elicit feedback from those you are interacting with. Albert Einstein famously said, 'Insanity is doing the same thing over and over and expecting a different result.' The most successful people in any profession are those who are willing to look critically at their own performance and, if necessary, reinvent themselves based upon what they find. Only through consciously taking ourselves through this learning cycle will we turn some theoretical concepts into practical skills.

Closure and implementation: summary box

- Always be looking for closure and get a gesture of commitment before you leave.
- Ensure that you have an implementation strategy.
- Understand the power balance but maximise your leverage to take you to closure.
- Don't take things personally and don't be drawn into the other party's game; use the emotional Aikido techniques to keep you focused on moving towards agreement.
- Review your processing to make your next negotiation even stronger.

In closing

Negotiation is about getting what you want in your life. Principled negotiation is about achieving that in a way that treats other people with respect and dignity. I said right at the beginning of this book that approaching negotiation from a principled point of view is worth doing because it works on lots of different levels. My hope is that you have also seen that it is a realistic system which allows you to deal with everybody, even those unscrupulous people that you may come across, but at the same time stay true to your own values and maintain self-respect without getting drawn into their game.

It may mean that you will have to break some of the conditioned patterns of thinking and behaving that are often taught. Be yourself but be open to building in some of the skills and techniques described here and the results should speak for themselves.

The negotiation teacher G. Richard Shell says that effective negotiation is 10% technique and 90% attitude and I hope that this message has come across through the things described here. How you approach the negotiation and the people you are negotiating with, mentally and emotionally, has much more to do with your outcomes than the simple mechanics of bargaining. This whole system is not about contriving to be something you are not; it is about understanding your own natural style and using that as a foundation to build upon. You will only become truly successful at this if you are being true to yourself, but at the same time, honing your skills to express yourself in the most constructive way possible.

If you look back at the questionnaire at the beginning of this book, that simple model made the assumption that people come from two broad directions when it comes to negotiations; the co-operative and the competitive. Whatever your starting point, it is possible to make some adjustments to that basic style so that your results are more consistent, effective and principled. My personal style was very naturally co-operative, but time and experience taught me to be a little more assertive about getting my interests satisfied and a little less openly trusting, particularly when it comes to dealing with strong competitive types.

Co-operative types can also set their expectations too low on occasions. This is because people with this style like to put the other person's needs ahead of their own. Often, once the bottom line has been achieved, the co-operative negotiator can relax and feel as though their needs have been satisfied. By not focusing on the bottom line, but by raising expectations and setting more ambitious, but nevertheless realistic goals, the co-operative negotiator will get much better results.

It is easy for co-operative types to think that com-promised relationships are a natural cost of achieving optimum results. You need to retrain yourself to realise that these two things are not mutually exclusive. It is possible for the co-operative negotiator to use their natural ability for positively managing the people issues and get what they want. Because they sometimes feel it is a little selfish or self-indulgent to set really high expectations, co-operative types should consider reframing and perhaps thinking in terms of negotiating on behalf of somebody else. If you think that the outcome of the bargaining process will directly affect your kids' university fund, your ability to provide for your family or your own retirement, it may put a bit more of an edge on your attitude as you enter the negotiation room.

Being aware that not everybody has the same style and is therefore not as trustworthy when it comes to following through on promises should lead you to asserting real commitment rather than just agreements at the end of the bargaining process. There is an old Sufi saying: 'Trust in God, but tie your camel first.' Again, just to be clear, this is not about changing your style from what is fundamentally natural to you. If you are a co-operative negotiator, you may have natural empathetic abilities and a level of sensitivity that will allow you to manage some of the people issues with considerable skill. This needs to be tempered with a greater level of assertiveness that will give you even better results.

On the other hand, if you are a naturally competitive negotiator your results will improve if you realise that satisfying the other party's needs can actually benefit you also. You will still feel the impulse to assert your own needs first, but perhaps rather than just thinking in terms of win, think in terms of win/win. One of the central points made in this book is that very often people want different things and it is in satisfying these differing interests that the best solutions lie. The competitive negotiator's frame of mind is very often in terms of 'more for you means less for me', but this can lead to missing the most profitable solution for everybody, or at least leaving something on the table. Only by slowing down and considering the other party's interests will you find that truly creative solution where more for them means more for you. Competitive negotiators tend to be very results- rather than process-orientated, but they must remember that managing the relationships is a key element in sustaining the most profitable results over time. Use your natural ability to set challenging targets and gain commitment, but balance that with how you manage the relationships because that will have a direct impact upon your personal reputation and will ultimately have a tangible effect on your results.

This active cultivation of your own style will allow you to build upon your natural abilities and at the same time strengthen your weak areas, giving a much more holistic approach to your negotiations. By balancing all of these things effectively you will be negotiating with integrity.

Many people approach negotiations with fear and trepidation and then either compromise their own interests to manage the relationship or take extreme positions to avoid being taken advantage of. Negotiating with integrity is another way altogether; it is about developing your communication skills sufficiently to remain open and gather as much information as possible; it is about getting behind positions and identifying interests and looking for creative ways of satisfying those interests even if the other party is not consciously aware of the process that you are taking them through. We said right at the beginning of the book that these are skills that can be applied in many areas of your life, not just in business. So, learning to negotiate well is also about being in control of your life. Life is in a constant state of flux; changing and expanding all the time and this is a fact that we cannot change. What we are in control of is the direction of that change, particularly that change that has a direct impact upon us. Learning to negotiate well will firmly put your hand on the tiller and help you to take more active control of the direction you wish to go in. So the skills described here go beyond simple application in the workplace. When I run workshops on this subject, the theory is useful only in so much as it provides a framework for learning. The words do not teach — experience alone does that — so only by going out and practising the techniques and principles described here will you create new habits and get improved results. Good luck.

Index